KINGDOM LIFESTYLE

THE *WORLDVIEW*

OF THE KINGDOM

OF GOD

Darrow L. Miller | Bob Moffitt | Scott D. Allen

YWAM
PUBLISHING
P.O. BOX 55787 SEATTLE, WA 98155

Disciple
Nations
Alliance
Founded by:
Harvest and Food for
the Hungry International

Howard

YWAM Publishing is the publishing ministry of Youth With A Mission. Youth With A Mission (YWAM) is an international missionary organization of Christians from many denominations dedicated to presenting Jesus Christ to this generation. To this end, YWAM has focused its efforts in three main areas: (1) training and equipping believers for their part in fulfilling the Great Commission (Matthew 28:19), (2) personal evangelism, and (3) mercy ministry (medical and relief work).

For a free catalog of books and materials, contact:

YWAM Publishing
P.O. Box 55787, Seattle, WA 98155
(425) 771-1153 or (800) 922-2143
www.ywampublishing.com

The Worldview of the Kingdom of God
Copyright © 2005 by Darrow L. Miller, Bob Moffitt, and Scott D. Allen

10 09 08 07 06 05   10 9 8 7 6 5 4 3 2 1

Published by Youth With A Mission Publishing
P.O. Box 55787
Seattle, WA 98155

ISBN 1-57658-351-1

Printed in the United States of America.

Kingdom Lifestyle Bible Studies

God's Remarkable Plan for the Nations
God's Unshakable Kingdom
The Worldview of the Kingdom of God

≈ Acknowledgments

This project has truly been a team effort. Many thanks to Randy Hoag, President of Food for the Hungry International, for his vision to develop this series and for his encouragement along the way. Grateful thanks to Max Rondoni for his invaluable assistance in helping us organize a great mass of written materials and lecture notes into something we could work with. A debt of gratitude goes to Cindy Benn and Natalie Clarke for their help with editing and proofreading. We also gratefully acknowledge the expert editorial assistance of Judith Couchman. Not only did she bring a degree of professionalism to the writing of these lessons, she brought her heart and encouragement as well. Several others have contributed valuable insights in shaping the content of these lessons. Among these are Karla Tesch, David Conner, Dave Evans, Rhonda McEwen, Arturo Cuba, and Gary Zander. We also thank Warren Walsh, Marit Newton, Richard Kim, Janice Manuel, and all the other professionals at YWAM Publishing for the considerable time and energy they put into the development of these books. What an honor and privilege it has been to work with such a wonderful team of committed brothers and sisters in Christ.

Contents

≈ Foreword

Greetings from a fellow pilgrim! I am so pleased that you are beginning this Bible study. My passion is to see people growing in their relationships with King Jesus and his kingdom. I pray that this book and learning process will be such a blessing to you.

The Kingdom Lifestyle series is based on the analogy of a tree. The Bible often uses the metaphor of a fruitful tree to describe a healthy Christian life. Jesus said, "[It] is to my Father's glory, that you bear much fruit, showing yourselves to be my disciples" (John 15:8). Psalm 1 describes a blessed man as one who "is like a tree planted by streams of water, which yields its fruit in season and whose leaf does not wither. Whatever he does prospers" (vs. 3). The "streams of water" represent God's Word, or "the law of the LORD" (vs. 2).

So it is with our lives. To bear abundant fruit, we need to be rooted in God's Word. Not only are we to delight in God's Word and meditate on it (Ps. 1:2), but we must apply it. The apostle James warns, "Do not merely listen to the word, and so deceive yourselves. Do what it says" (James 1:22). In the strength that Christ provides, we are to conform every aspect of our lives to God's Word. It should shape our relationships with Christ, our vocational lives, our relationships with family members and fellow believers, and our ministries to our communities, nations, and the world.

This is what the Kingdom Lifestyle series is all about. It's about helping you deepen your relationship with the awesome, glorious God who is King of the universe and increase your knowledge of his powerful Word. And it's about assisting you in living out every facet of your life based on this relationship and knowledge. Ultimately, it's about bearing good fruit to the glory of God. No life can compare with the joyful, peace-filled, purposeful life lived for God, in his strength and according to his Word.

This particular study, *The Worldview of the Kingdom of God*, explores what it means to think "Christianly" about every aspect of life and then live a life consistent with this perspective. According to respected evangelical scholar and theologian John Stott, "A mind which has firmly grasped the basic presuppositions of Scripture and is thoroughly informed with biblical truth...can think with Christian integrity about the problems of the contemporary world. [It can] think about even the most 'secular' topics 'Christianly,' that is, from a Christian perspective."[1]

What are the major themes and presuppositions of Scripture? What is the "big story" the Bible tells? If we take a bird's-eye view of the whole of Scripture, we see that God has supernaturally woven its various individual books together to form a single meta-story. This big story of the Bible can be divided into four major stages: the Creation, the Fall, the Redemption, and the Consummation. This story provides us with a comprehensive Christian worldview. Like all worldviews, the biblical worldview answers life's big questions: What is ultimately real? Who is man? What is the purpose of human existence? Where is history going? Yet only the biblical worldview answers these questions from the perspective of God—the Creator and Lord of the universe.

Thinking "Christianly" is essential to being Christ's disciples. If, as Christians, we fail to think and act intentionally from a Christian worldview, we will by default think and act according to the predominant belief systems of our surrounding cultures, with consequences destructive to our faith as well as our ability to change our societies. I pray that this study will help you live intentionally, moment by moment, on the basis of the presuppositions of Scripture in every area of your life—the very essence of being the salt and light that Jesus challenged us to be.

May grace and joy abound in your life.

Serving the King and the kingdom together,
—Randy Hoag
President, Food for the Hungry International

About This Study

In this study, you'll learn about the biblical worldview—the worldview of the kingdom of God—and why understanding it, putting it on, and living it out are essential to living a fruitful, abundant life—a life that God can effectively use to transform the nations. You can study by yourself or with a small group. There are eight sessions in this study.

Theme of Each Session

Session 1. We'll define *worldview* and learn that ideas have consequences. Your worldview largely determines how you live, how you function with your family, how you view your work, and the role you'll play in society.

Session 2. We'll examine how worldviews operate around the world. Each society embraces a dominant worldview that the majority of its people believe. Worldviews spread geographically and penetrate deep into the fabric of society. Despite the wide variety of worldviews in the world, the Bible teaches that there is only one true worldview. As we "put on" the biblical worldview, we see the world and our lives as they truly are.

Session 3. We'll begin to examine the biblical worldview in greater depth. At its core is the infinite, yet personal God who created everything and whose real existence defines all reality.

Session 4. We'll discover what the Bible teaches about human life. We'll learn that all human life is created by God and endowed with inherent worth and dignity. Human life is sacred. We'll also discover that work is sacred because God works and we are made in his image. He has given us the task of working in his "garden" and caring for it. Finally, we'll see that men and women, in their natural, unredeemed states, stand in rebellion against God.

Session 5. We'll explore what the Bible has to say about creation. God is the creator of the physical world. He existed before it did and "spoke" it into existence. God created the natural world with the capacity to grow and expand. For example, a single tree has the potential to expand into an entire forest, and people can use their creativity to study creation and discover new resources. Men and women are also commanded to exercise authority over nature. This biblical authority is not domination, but stewardship and care. We are to protect, conserve, and cherish God's creation.

Session 6. We'll look at the biblical view of history. God is the author of history, so it has meaning and purpose. The Bible is the record of God's unfolding redemptive plan in history. Each human life has astounding significance because God uses individuals to unfold this history-encompassing plan. He has given each person unique talents and gifts for this very purpose.

Session 7. We'll examine how Satan, "the father of lies," opposes the biblical worldview by distorting it. These distortions take the form of false worldviews. When lies are believed, they impact individuals and nations. Satan's lies penetrate customs, practices, institutions, social structures, and laws. Only God's truth can bring release, freedom, and healing.

Session 8. We'll focus on practical ways you can put on and live out a life based on the biblical worldview. We'll learn that "putting off" false beliefs and "putting on" the truth does not happen automatically at conversion. It is a lifelong process that requires disciplined study of God's Word. As we engage in this process, our minds are transformed, and transformed minds naturally lead to a transformation in our behavior and, ultimately, our entire lives. We are to be "salt and light" by taking the biblical worldview out into our neighborhoods, communities, and nations. As we do, our cultures are transformed and our nations are discipled.

Sections of Each Session

Key Words to Know. After the opening narrative, each session includes discussion of some of the key words found in the session. In addition to reading the provided definitions, you may wish to use additional resources, such as a Bible dictionary or commentary, for further study of these terms. Understanding these words will help you get the most out of the study.

Key Verses to Read. After the discussion of key words, you'll find a key Scripture passage for the session. Carefully read the quotation and answer the questions after it. These key verses provide a biblical framework for the central teaching of each session. Whether you're leading or participating in a small group or studying alone, you can consult the suggested responses for each session's Key Verses to Read questions in the Study Notes at the end of the book. Not all questions have a "right" or "wrong" answer, but these suggestions will help stimulate your thinking.

Biblical Insights. This narrative section is the heart of each session. Carefully read it, taking notes as you go along. As you read, highlight meaningful or important points and write down questions that come to mind.

Discovery Questions. This section is designed to take you into God's Word for a deeper understanding of the material covered in the Biblical Insights section. Suggested responses to these questions can be found in the Study Notes at the back of the book.

Key Points to Remember. This section briefly summarizes the key points for each session.

Closing Thoughts. This section provides a wrap-up of the session, designed to transition from the main body of the session to the personal application that follows.

Personal Application. Here's where the study gets personal. These questions are designed to help you reflect on your own life and experiences and move you toward personal application.

A Practical Response. The optional activities suggested at the end of the session will help you tangibly apply the biblical teachings presented in that lesson.

If you're leading a small group through this study, before beginning please read the Leader's Guide. Guidelines are provided that will help you enhance your group's effectiveness.

Please join us as we delve into Scripture and discover the power and beauty of the biblical worldview—the only worldview that describes reality as it truly exists, as God created it, the only worldview that leads to life and provides a foundation for free, just, and compassionate societies.

The Transforming Power of Truth

But be on your guard against the yeast
of the Pharisees and Sadducees.
—*Matthew 16:11*

It happened during my second year in Japan where I was serving as a twenty-three-year-old missionary. I'd traveled abroad before, but this was the first time I'd actually moved to a foreign country, and like most people who live abroad, the experience allowed me to reflect on how deeply my native culture had influenced me. The contrast between my everyday life and that of the Japanese people I encountered brought a number of my assumptions to the surface, and much of what I was seeing for the first time, I didn't like. I began to realize that my life was not shaped so much by biblical truth as it was by a particular set of modern American values.

Jesus had a word for mental assumptions that pollute our perceptions. That word is "yeast." Jesus warned his disciples in Matthew 16:11–12 to beware of the "yeast of the Pharisees and Sadducees." The Pharisees and Sadducees were the leading religious and philosophic teachers of their time. They formed the cultural elite, whose teachings played a major role in shaping Jewish society. As yeast penetrates a lump of dough, so the teachings of the Pharisees and Sadducees had penetrated and impacted

11

the culture the disciples lived in. It was their influence that was insidi-
ously and powerfully shaping the disciples' view of the world, without
their even realizing it. Jesus was saying, in effect, "though you read the
scriptures and though you walk with me, you are being influenced by
worldly ideas to such an extent that you are failing to understand the
important lessons I'm trying to teach you. Beware!"[1]

Just as it did the disciples, the worldly "yeast" of our culture shapes all
of us in ways we often fail to recognize. Each of us carries around a mental model of the world, a set of ideas or assumptions about what we
believe to be true and false, wrong and right. These assumptions shape
our choices and ultimately determine the kind of lives we lead. As someone raised in late-twentieth-century America, I've been influenced by
values such as rugged individualism, moral relativism, consumerism, and
an overarching need for personal comfort and self-indulgence. The
longer I lived in Japan, the more I reckoned with these values. Through
this spiritual crisis, I realized that my faith needed adjustment. It had to
be more than my personal relationship with Jesus. It had to be more than
church attendance, Bible study, and even works of charity. While all
these elements are important to a healthy Christian life, they are not
enough. I came to see that "genuine Christianity is a way of seeing and
comprehending all reality. It is a worldview."[2]

The basis for the biblical worldview is God's revelation in Scripture.
It teaches us that, "Everything that exists came into being at God's command and is therefore subject to him, finding its purpose and meaning in
him. The implication is that in every topic we investigate, from ethics to
economics to ecology, the truth is found only in relationship to God and
his revelation."[3] As the early fathers of the church used to say, "all truth
is God's truth."

Humans are social beings. We develop our mind-sets—our ways of
seeing the world—from our cultures. We tend to think the way our cultures think and value what our cultures value. This is part of what it
means to be human.

However, when we accept Christ as Savior, our mind-sets need to be
renewed. The word *repent*—from the Greek word *metanoeo*—means to

change one's mind. Repentance results in seeing the world the way God created it, then living within that framework. We are to have the mind of Christ (1 Cor. 2:16). We are to "take captive every thought to make it obedient to Christ" (2 Cor. 10:5). We are to "not conform any longer to the pattern of this world, but be transformed by the renewing of [our] mind" (Rom. 12:2). In coming to Christ, we need to begin to think "Christianly." We need to increasingly take on the mind of Christ, not the mind we inherit from our culture.

Understanding Christianity as a worldview is important, not just for us personally, but for our society and the nations of this world as well. This has never been more important than it is today. The past 150 years have witnessed an unprecedented missionary movement aimed at preaching the gospel and planting churches among the "least reached" of the world. Largely, this movement has been successful at what it set out to do—save souls and plant churches. Today there are more churches and more Christians in the world than at any time in history. But to what end? Poverty and corruption thrive in developing countries that have been evangelized. Moral and spiritual poverty reign in the "Christian" West. In many parts of the world where the church is growing, the growth is a mile wide and an inch deep. It has lost its characteristics of being salt and light in society (Matt. 5:13–16).

The famous church father Augustine recognized that "a people's dominant worldview inevitably shapes the world they have in view."[4] According to the Bible, God's archenemy, Satan, deceives not only individuals but entire nations as well (Rev. 20:3). His lies are the ultimate source of all the suffering, corruption, and poverty we see in our own culture and around the world. But the church can counteract Satan's lies by telling the truth.

After his resurrection, Jesus met with his disciples and said to them: "All authority in heaven and on earth has been given to me." He then commanded them to "make disciples of all nations" by going, baptizing, and teaching (Matt. 28:18–20). Because Jesus is both Creator and Lord over everything, his command to make disciples is far more than a mandate to simply "tell" the nations about Jesus. We must demonstrate the reality of Jesus' Lordship through our lives, families, vocations, communities, and cultures. We must teach the world the entirety of the biblical worldview. The truth must not only change lives, but transform cultures as well.

In the words of Christian author and activist Charles Colson, "God cares not only about redeeming souls, but also about restoring his creation.... Our job is not only to build up the church but also to build a society to the glory of God."[5]

What Is a Worldview?

Josie was a Peace Corps worker and nurse at the Serabu Mission Hospital in Sierra Leone, a nation on the west coast of Africa. She had just completed teaching a course in microbiology to ten Sierra Leonean nursing students. All the students had passed their examinations. In doing so, they had demonstrated an understanding that viruses, bacteria, and other microscopic organisms cause disease.

After the class discussed the results of the final exam, one student raised her hand and said, "Miss Josie, I know what you taught us about how white people get sick, but do you want to know how people *really* get sick?"

"How?"

"It's the *witches*! They are invisible and fly around at night, biting people's backs!"

Josie later explained, "At that moment, with a heaviness of heart, I realized that—as far as the Sierra Leonean students were concerned—I didn't know what I was talking about when it came to the cause of disease. Their grandmothers had taught them that witches were real and that microorganisms were what white people believed in."[1]

Josie and her nursing students operated from different sets of assumptions regarding the cause of disease. Each set of assumptions was part of its holder's worldview, or "belief system." Josie believed in a physical cause of disease; her students believed in a spiritual or supernatural cause. While the manifestation of any particular disease was the same, Josie and her students had different understandings of its nature and cause. Their respective beliefs were rooted in different worldviews and created conflicting ideas about how to cure diseases.

In this session you'll learn more about worldviews—what they are, how they work, and why understanding and examining them is so crucial for followers of Jesus.

KEY WORDS TO KNOW

Defining Worldview

Assumption (assume)

To *assume* is to believe a concept or viewpoint without thinking critically about it. It is to take something for granted. We each make assumptions about many things, and such beliefs can be held consciously or unconsciously.

Worldview

A worldview is the total set of assumptions that a person holds, either consciously or unconsciously, about the world and how it works.[2] It is sometimes referred to as a "belief system" or "mind-set." We typically acquire our worldviews in childhood and youth, yet later in life we rarely examine the assumptions that comprise it.

Reality

Reality is simply what truly exists and how it all actually works. The term encompasses both the natural and supernatural realms—*all* that is. *Reality* means the ultimate facts of existence, not just what we think we know or see, assume to be true, or wish were true. Our own understanding of reality is always conditional and subject to change over time; it is limited by our human ability to understand, by our present state of knowledge, and by what sources we have or accept for our views. Believers understand that true reality comes from the nature and will of our Creator and Sustainer.

The theologian Paul Tillich wrote about God as Ultimate Reality. Thus, when we accept God as Lord of our lives, we are also committing ourselves to lives based on this actual reality, not lesser standards for trust, understanding, or determining right choices.

KEY VERSES TO READ
With All Your Heart and Mind

Hearing that Jesus had silenced the Sadducees, the Pharisees got together. One of them, an expert in the law, tested him with this question: "Teacher, which is the greatest commandment in the Law?"

Jesus replied: "'Love the Lord your God with all your heart and with all your soul and with all your mind.' This is the first and greatest commandment. And the second is like it: 'Love your neighbor as yourself.' All the Law and the Prophets hang on these two commandments."

—*Matthew 22:34–40*

1. What is the greatest commandment upon which the entire law hangs?

   Love the Lord my God with all my heart and with all my soul and with all my mind

2. What do you think it means to love God with all your heart?

   I don't really know - knowing what to do in our mind and acting on it -

3. What do you think it means to love God with all your mind?

   As far as I can think - conciously & unconciously, knowingly & unawares — from God's world view

4. Why is it important to love God with both heart and mind?

   If we love Him with only our heart we become too spiritual & only our mind we become legalistical

BIBLICAL INSIGHTS
Eyeglasses for the Mind

Like Josie and her nursing students, each of us possesses a worldview. These worldviews shape our choices and how we live. According to scholar Samuel Huntington, "In the back of our minds are hidden assumptions...that determine how we perceive reality, what facts we look at, and how we judge their importance and merits."[3] These hidden assumptions also determine "what we believe is real and true, right and wrong, good and beautiful."[4] For this reason, understanding our world-views is both practical and important.

Our worldviews literally form who we are. These beliefs are deeply ingrained in our minds, and unearthing them is not easy. In many instances we remain unconscious of their existence or influence until alternative views challenge them. Nevertheless, a critical issue for any

follower of Jesus is whether or not his or her worldview is rooted in biblical truth or if instead the surrounding culture has shaped those beliefs.

In many ways our worldviews function like eyeglasses for the mind. We wear them all the time, and they shape and color everything we see. They focus our attention upon certain issues while filtering out others. Josie's world-view focused her attention on the physical causes of disease—the microscopic organisms that negatively affect the cell life of a human body. At the same time, her worldview tended to filter out possible spiritual causes for disease. Meanwhile, the worldview of her Sierra Leonean nursing students did the opposite.

As we grow and develop, others impart their assumptions about reality to us. Our beliefs are shaped by input from parents, friends, teachers, mentors, and role models. The broader culture we live in also influences our worldviews, which we absorb as we go about our daily lives, through sources like television and radio, what we read, the music we listen to, and even conversations with others.

The Big Questions of Life

Worldviews are extremely important, partly because they help answer "the big questions of life." For example: Does God exist, and if so, what is he like, or are we alone in an impersonal universe? Are there many gods, and if so, what are they like, and how do they relate to us? Who am I, and what is the purpose of my life? How should I understand the natural world around me? Is there purpose to history, or is it meaningless? Is history ultimately going somewhere, and if so, where? What happens after I die? Why is there so much pain and suffering in the world?

Imagine that you are a farmer who has worked all season to raise a crop, but the rains never fall and your crop fails. You might ask, "Why is this happening?" Or imagine you are a parent and your child is killed in an auto accident. You might ask, "If God is good, how could he allow this to happen?" Your worldview answers these questions.

Interestingly, wherever one travels in the world, the big questions of life are basically the same. However, the answers vary tremendously. That is because they are founded upon different assumptions about life.

Ideas Reap Consequences

One of the purposes of this study is to provide you with an opportunity—perhaps for the first time—to examine your own worldview. Our hope is that you will take off your worldview glasses, handle them a bit, and examine them carefully. This is a powerful exercise—one of the most important exercises you can ever do! Your worldview is not simply a set of ideas floating through your head, with no bearing on the rest of your life. Rather, your worldview largely determines how you live, how you function within your family, the role you play in your community, and the type of society and nation you create with others.

You can compare a worldview to the roots of a fruit tree. We cannot see the roots. They exist below the ground. Yet they determine the kind of fruit the tree will produce. Jesus used this analogy to warn us against the teachings of false prophets.

> Watch out for false prophets. They come to you in sheep's clothing, but inwardly they are ferocious wolves. By their

fruit you will recognize them. Do people pick grapes from thornbushes, or figs from thistles? Likewise every good tree bears good fruit, but a bad tree bears bad fruit. A good tree cannot bear bad fruit, and a bad tree cannot bear good fruit. Every tree that does not bear good fruit is cut down and thrown into the fire. Thus, by their fruit you will recognize them.

—*Matthew 7:15–20*

Objective truth is recorded in the pages of Scripture. Yet Jesus warns us that lies also exist, and often they are subtle and difficult to detect. They arrive through "false prophets," who "come in sheep's clothing, but inwardly, they are ferocious wolves." Jesus also tells us that there is a direct link between false ideas (the roots) and the result or consequence of these false ideas in everyday life (the fruit). If our roots are formed according to God's truth, the fruit of our lives will reflect that truth and be good, a positive addition to our world. On the other hand, if our lives are the outgrowth of roots formed by lies, our fruit can only be more of the same, without worth and fit only to be discarded.

Just as people who look at a tree do not see the roots, those who observe our everyday lives and actions cannot see our worldviews. Like the roots of the fruit tree, our worldviews exist below the surface of our lives. Yet also like the roots of the fruit tree, our worldviews produce fruit that has the same character as the worldview itself. The things we value, the decisions we make, and our daily actions reflect and grow from the assumptions we hold about the big questions of life.

In short, our worldviews produce a certain kind of fruit, or consequences, in our everyday lives. A healthy worldview—one based on biblical truth—produces productive consequences. An unhealthy world-view—one based on lies—produces destructive consequences. These consequences not only affect our own lives, but also the lives of the people around us. This is even more reason to examine our own worldviews with care.

DISCOVERY QUESTIONS

A Shift in Perspective

The Bible teaches that we are "born again" (John 3:3–16) when we accept the good news of Christ by faith. Yet knowing and trusting Jesus for our salvation does not necessarily mean we immediately possess a comprehensive, biblical worldview. The process of renewing our minds with the truth is a lifelong process.

It was no different for Jesus' disciples, and they walked and talked with Jesus every day! In this session, you will examine one instance when the disciples' false worldview assumptions conflicted with the truth.

1. Read Mark 10:32–45. What is the setting of this discussion? What is about to happen?

   They, the disciples, are on their way to Jerusalem and Jesus is about to be arrested →

2. What did James and John want Christ to do for them? (vss. 35–37)

   They wanted to be 2nd in authority under Jesus they wanted to be close to Jesus

3. Why couldn't Christ grant their request? (vss. 38–40)

   It was not His place to give something that had probably already been set.

4. How did the other disciples react? (v. 41)

   they were greatly displeased with them

5. What is the world's standard of greatness? (v. 42)

   In the world the rulers are obeyed — have authority

6. What is Christ's standard of greatness? (vss. 43–44)
    To be great be a servant

7. What is one thing Christ did not come to earth to do? (v. 45)
    Jesus did not come to be served

8. What two things did he come to do? (v. 45)
    To serve and give His life a ransom

9. The disciples saw things from one perspective, a self-focused one, and Jesus saw them from quite another, from the perspective of reality. In the grid below, identify the perspectives of each worldview, drawing from Mark 10:32–45. Feel free to use your knowledge of other Scripture passages as well.

	The Disciples' View	**Jesus' View (Reality)**
Who is Christ?	*Master Rabboni*	*Servant*
What is the kingdom?	*Authority*	*Service*
What will the disciples' future lives be like?	*Rulers with authority*	*In Service to others*
How should we live?	*Get the most we can*	*be the best servant we can*

10. From your knowledge of Scripture, describe some events that occurred in the disciples' lives that challenged their false worldview and brought it into alignment with reality. For help, see Luke 24:13–34, John 4:5–42, Matthew 14:13–20, Matthew 15:1–20, John 13:1–17.

In Luke 24 Jesus revealed Himself to the disciples they saw who He was. The woman at the well saw who Jesus was in reality to who she was. The pharisees were stuck in their own worldview

KEY POINTS TO REMEMBER

A Worldview Review

1. A worldview is the total set of assumptions that a person holds, either consciously or unconsciously, about the world and how it works.
2. All of us have worldviews. They are deeply ingrained in our minds.
3. A worldview helps us answer the "big questions of life."
4. A worldview largely determines how we live, how we function in our families, how we view our work, and the roles we play in society.

CLOSING THOUGHTS

Discipleship of the Mind

According to author and scholar James Sire, "A worldview is a map of reality; and like any map, it may fit what is actually there, or it may be [very] misleading. The map is not the world itself of course, only an image of it, more or less accurate in some places, distorted in others. Still, all of us carry around such a map in our mental makeup and we act upon it. All our thinking presupposes it. Most of our experience fits into it."[5]

There is only one map that accurately reflects reality as it truly exists. This "map" is the biblical worldview. The entire world is the Lord's. He created it all. Loving God with your entire mind means seeking to understand everything in light of God's revealed truth in Scripture. It means working toward "understanding God's ordinances for all of creation, for the natural world, for societies, for businesses, for schools, for the government, for science, and for the arts."[6]

It means developing a biblical worldview, and this is a rewarding, enriching journey for a disciple of Christ.

PERSONAL APPLICATION
What's Your View?

Use these questions to apply the lesson's principles as you continue your journey of developing a biblical worldview and loving God with all of your mind.

1. Think of a time when someone challenged elements of your worldview with a different worldview. Perhaps it was a friend or family member who is not a Christian or someone from a different country or cultural background. How did you respond? How did this help you become more aware of your own worldview?

    In Japan shoes are dirty so you don't wear them inside I struggled to change because I wore work boots but now I wear shoes that slip on or off easily

2. Is there one or more of the big questions of life that you wrestle with? How does your worldview inform your answers to these questions?

    No, God IS in control!

3. Think of a person who holds a worldview different from your own. How would he or she answer the big questions of life?

    Japanese generally don't believe maybe since there is no God "I am in control" lack of discipline also causes people to have a harder time to come to chi

4. Consider the impact made on your life by family members, teachers, peers, authority figures, the media (books, television, movies, music, magazines), cultural events and celebrations, and religious traditions.

What have been some of the biggest influences in your life toward shaping your worldview? Describe how this influence occurred.

My mom made us go to church when we were young

5. Take a moment and reflect on the "fruit" that your worldview has produced in your life. What are some of the "good fruits"? Can you trace these good fruits back to foundational worldview assumptions? If so, what are they?

giving — going into missions

6. What about the "bad fruits" in your life? List them, and describe the worldview assumptions that influenced them.

I use to read playboy magazine I'm not sure how strong the hold of these are but they influence my thinking + value of women

7. With God's help, how can you minimize future bad fruits?

trust Him more - follow His ways better.

8 -6

A PRACTICAL RESPONSE
What Is Your Country's View?

What generally accepted assumptions and values shape your country's worldview? Create a chart like the one below, adding other relevant categories if you wish. Describe how you think most people in your country view each issue or topic. If people in your country hold diverse opinions, list the major ones. If you'd rather, you can express your country's views with descriptive photos or drawings rather than words.

When you've finished, review each category and express your feelings about the assumptions and values you identified. Then compare your personal values and assumptions to your country's views. How do they coincide? How do they differ? Why?

Choose one viewpoint that you could influence positively in the next month. For example, if people in your country think poorly of other countries, what could you do to better educate yourself and others about the positive attributes of another country?

Issues or Topics	Generally accepted values and assumptions of your country
Appearance	Depends on who — hippie's or Amway Christian ① God looks on the inner man not outer
Prov 31 Eph 6:1 Family Life Eph 6:	In the '50's and earlier family was very important. nowadays not as much - ie. divorce
John 8:32 I Pet 2:15-17 Freedom I Cor 10:23	I think most people take their freedom for granted today -
Is 9:6 Rom 13:1-2 Government I Pet 2:13-	America is always right the best
Matt 6:25-34 Health I Cor 12:7	In Am. health is generally taken for granted.
Gen 12:3 Other Countries 2 Chron 6:32-33	We Americans think other countries should learn Eng.
Eph 3:20 Lk 6:38 Prosperity Matt 6:19-21	I have the right to have all my needs met.
James 1:26 I Tim 4:7 Religion John 4:23-24	I'm free to believe what I want
Gal 5:22-24 Success Eph 1:3-6.	I can do all things —
Phil 3:7 Work Eph	Work hard, you'll get ahead I can do all things —

(margin note, right of Freedom row) freedom in God Lay down our right Phil 2:6

(margin note, left of Prosperity row) Phil 4:12

The next session: *exploring worldviews in action*

Worldviews at Work in the World

In early nineteenth-century America, churches were so involved in charitable activity that they "were said to be promoting a 'Benevolent Empire.'"[1] Countless Christian charities served the poor by meeting their material and physical needs and by distributing tracts and Bibles.

Biblical beliefs underscored most of this activity. Christians worshiped a God who, through death on a cross, exhibited the literal meaning of compassion: *suffering together with another.* As a result, many Christians gave wholeheartedly of themselves and "suffered together with" the poor. They sacrificed in gratitude for the suffering of God on their behalf and in obedience to biblical teaching. They worshiped a God who showed compassion and at the same time demanded change, so they also labored toward the spiritual and personal transformation of the people they served.

But beginning in the 1840s, things began to change. One of the first challenges to this charity consensus came from the nation's leading journalist of the time, Horace Greeley. Greeley worked as the founder and editor of the *New York Tribune.* Contrary to biblical teaching, Greeley believed that "the heart of man is not depraved, that his passions do not prompt to wrongdoing, and do not therefore by their actions produce evil."[2] He also believed that poverty could end by redistributing wealth from the rich to the poor so that all receive an equal share. According to Greeley, "evil flows only from social repression. [If people] are allowed full scope, free play, and perfect and complete development, then universal happiness must be the result.... Create a new form of society in which this shall be possible...then you will have a perfect society; then you will have the Kingdom of Heaven."[3]

These new ideas entered the mainstream American society through a series of newspaper debates that Greeley conducted with Henry Raymond, a devout Christian and the founder of the *New York Times*. For Raymond, Greeley's ideas were "in the most direct hostility to the doctrines of the Bible. [They] recognize no absolute distinction between right and wrong.... [They are] the exact [opposite] of Christianity; [they] start from opposite fundamental principles and aim at precisely opposite results."[4]

Through this public debate, Greeley effectively won over many of his journalistic colleagues, who in turn promoted his ideas through their newspapers. Over time, Greeley's ideas became dominant and influenced the culture. Americans increasingly saw poverty as rooted not in individual human sinfulness on the part of rich and poor alike but in larger, impersonal, social and structural inequalities. The solution became political rather than spiritual, and political power was seen as the primary means for advancing toward a just society. As Greeley implied, the perfect society was achievable through enlightened government policy and the creation of new social structures and programs. The ultimate solution to eliminating poverty belonged to the government, which held the power to tax citizens and redistribute wealth from the rich to the poor.

By the 1960s this notion that government was the solution had so firmly taken root within American culture that a 1964 economic report to President Johnson boasted that "the elimination of poverty is well within the means of federal, state, and local governments."[5] Such thinking resulted in an explosion of government welfare programs. From then on, billions of dollars were spent on this government War on Poverty. At the same time, the people receiving government welfare swelled from 4.3 million in 1965 to 10.8 million by 1974.[6]

Over time, private, church-based charity efforts dramatically decreased. Many Christians began to believe that caring for the poor was not their responsibility, but that of the government. But perhaps the darkest legacy of this welfare experiment centered on the lost motivation, vision, and dependency it created among the poor. The welfare system harmed the poor by reducing them from human beings to mouths to be fed. The Christian idea of compassion—of suffering together with—dwindled. Compassion was reduced to a weak feeling of pity that carried no call for personal involvement in the lives of the poor.

This session explores how worldviews affect cultures and societies. Over time the dominant worldview of society may change as new beliefs replace old ones. This change can be accompanied by dramatic and often unintended social shifts.

Matt 14: 14
9 36

KEY WORDS TO KNOW

Mk 6: 34

A Look at Dominant Worldviews

Lk 1: 41
7: 13
Mt 20:34

Culture/Society

The word *culture* derives from the Latin word *cultus*, which means *habitation, tilling, refinement,* or *worship*. From it we get the English word *cult*. Though we now often use the word more narrowly, to describe something false or offbeat, its basic meaning is a system of religious worship, based on particular beliefs. (Sometimes archaeologists simply use the Latin word instead.) Building on this definition, a culture is a particular pattern of thought, speech, and behavior that stems from deeply held beliefs about the nature of reality. These patterns, covering most aspects of a people's lives, pass from one generation to the next. It is in this sense that we speak of "Japanese culture" or "Latin culture." Cultures alter over time because the religious beliefs at their core change.

The word *society* has a similar definition. A society is the union of people into a community or nation. The majority shares a common purpose, traditions, core assumptions about reality, and patterns of behavior.

Dominant

The word *dominant* is an adjective used to describe that which exerts the greatest influence. For example, the dominant voice in a room of people is the one heard over the rest. In this session, the word describes a society's prevailing set of beliefs.

KEY VERSES TO READ

Deceptive Philosophies

> See to it that no one takes you captive through hollow and deceptive philosophy, which depends on human tradition and the basic principles of this world rather than on Christ.
>
> —*Colossians 2:8*

1. The word *philosophy* comes from two Greek words: *phileo*, which means love, and *sophia*, which means wisdom. So *philosophy* means to love wisdom. What do the following verses say about wisdom?

    Proverbs 2:6 *The Lord gives wisdom*

    Proverbs 3:13 *a man who finds wisdom is happy (blessed)*

2. Based on the verses from Proverbs, how should a Christian regard wisdom? *wisdom is a blessing from God*

3. Colossians 2:8 refers to *worldly* philosophy. What words does Paul use to describe it?

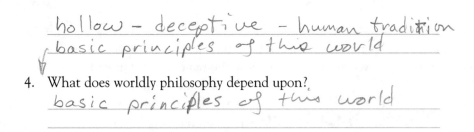

hollow – deceptive – human tradition
– basic principles of this world

4. What does worldly philosophy depend upon?

basic principles of this world

5. What do you think Paul means by "the basic principles of this world"?

note 24

BIBLICAL INSIGHTS

The Impact of Worldviews on Society

In every society there exists a dominant worldview shared by the majority. However, this doesn't mean that each person in the society ascribes equally to this dominant worldview. There are always people who hold minority beliefs.

Still, the dominant worldview of a society tends to wield the most influence in shaping its culture and institutions. It determines which things the society does and does not value. It is evident through the society's educational, political, social, religious, legal, and economic institutions. It also resonates through media and popular culture.

The dominant worldview of our society influences us profoundly. Often we do not realize this until we leave our society and visit another one. Then we begin to understand—sometimes with amazement—how strongly we hold to our society's dominant worldview.

Worldviews on the Move

Worldviews are constantly on the move. They spread outward across oceans and around the world. A classic example is the spread of Christianity. Jesus commanded his followers to be "my witnesses in Jerusalem, and in all Judea and Samaria, and to the ends of the earth" (Acts 1:8). From Jerusalem, Christianity spread to every continent and nearly every nation on earth.

Worldviews often originate in the minds of intellectuals, philosophers, and theologians. From there, artists and musicians illustrate them. (It has been said, if you want to know how the next generation will live, study the art and music of today.) Worldviews then spread to other educated or professional people, such as teachers, lawyers, pastors, journalists, and politicians. Eventually they can become "institutionalized" as laws, governing policies, and educational curricula. As they continue to penetrate a culture, they eventually affect the everyday behavior and lifestyle of its people.

Ideas Spread Through Culture

The Intellectuals
Religion, Philosophy

The Balladeers
Popular Music, the Arts

The Professionals
Law, Politics, Economics

The Common People
Popular Culture, the Public

Worldviews also spread through time, from one generation to the next. They pass from parents to children. In the Old Testament, God instructed parents of his chosen nation, Israel, to accurately teach his revealed commands and laws from generation to generation. This would ensure that the true knowledge of God would not be lost or forgotten (Deut. 4:1–10).

A Diversity of Worldviews

Throughout history there has been—and will continue to be—a wide range of worldviews. In this study we organize this broad range into three general worldview categories.

Naturalism. Naturalism (sometimes referred to as secularism or materialism) encompasses a set of beliefs that denies or ignores the existence of spiritual reality. According to naturalism, the physical universe is all that exists. There is no God, or gods, and no spirit within human beings. All phenomena in the world can be explained through the science-defined "laws" (or principles) governing the physical universe and chance combinations and interactions of matter.

Today naturalism is the dominant worldview in much of the industrialized West. It gained supremacy through the widespread acceptance of British botanist Charles Darwin's (1809–1882) theory of natural evolution. Naturalism underpins the modern faiths of scientism and postmodernism.

| *Naturalism's View* | *Animism's View* | *Theism's View* |

Animism. Sometimes referred to as pantheism, animism is a set of beliefs that sees the world as full of (or animated with) spiritual beings. There are scores of gods, demons, and angels. In fact, according to animism, ultimate reality is fundamentally spiritual. The line separating physical and spiritual reality is very weak or nonexistent, with spirits inhabiting rocks, trees, and other elements of nature. The gods of animism may be expressed as impersonal forces or as personal, even humanlike, beings. Their actions are often arbitrary and unpredictable. Animism underpins many ancient religions such as Shinto in Japan and Hinduism in India and is still dominant in many less industrialized societies in Africa, Latin America, and Asia. In addition, elements of the modern New Age movement in the West have also adopted some animistic concepts.

Theism. Though the word can have other shades of meaning, in this study it will mean the belief in *one* God who is the all-powerful creator of the physical universe. According to theism, reality is comprised of both physical and spiritual reality. The physical universe exists, but so does God who created and sustains it and who has a real existence apart from it. Likewise, human life is an inseparable combination of a physical body and a spirit. Theism contrasts with naturalism in that its proponents believe that God exists. Theism contrasts with animism in that there is only *one* all-powerful creator God, rather than many spirits controlling events. Judaism, Islam, and Christianity are the three major world religions that subscribe to this general belief.

While it's helpful to understand these three worldview categories as distinct from one another, it's common for people and societies to combine elements from each. Typically, one of these categories will be dominant within a culture; however, there will likely be elements of all three categories evident to some degree. In the industrialized West for example, naturalism is the dominant worldview, yet Christianity continues to exert an influence. Likewise, the animistic beliefs espoused by some in the New Age movement are exerting an increasing influence. In addition, today many Europeans are rediscovering and worshiping the same pagan gods that their ancient ancestors once worshiped.

The Biblical Worldview

While there is a diversity of beliefs among the world's peoples, the Bible declares that there is only one *true* reality. If this is the case, then there can be only one worldview that reflects the truth. The challenge for us is to understand this worldview and order our lives according to it.

This true worldview—the biblical worldview—is God's revelation to us in Scripture and through creation. The Bible teaches that this worldview is actually embedded within the hearts of all people (Rom. 2:14–15), though humanity's fallen nature diminishes its presence.

When our minds embrace the biblical worldview, we begin to see the world as it really is—as God created and sustains it. As we believe and act on this worldview, our lives manifest healthy, fruitful living. This will be good not only for us but for our families, communities, and societies as well.

The Bible teaches that human nature is not perfect, but fallen. Because of fallen human nature, we cannot clearly see true reality without God's help. Naturalism, animism, and some forms of theism are distortions of the truth that prevent us from clearly viewing all of reality. Either they allow us to see a portion of what is real or they distort the portion that we see. Often, they do both. The biblical worldview, by contrast, allows us to see all that is real. When we "put on" the biblical worldview, we can understand God as he truly is—and ourselves and creation as we were made to be.

DISCOVERY QUESTIONS
The Truth Sets You Free

Open your Bible to learn more about truth and how to respond to it.

1. Begin by reading Isaiah 45:18–19 and John 17:17. How do these verses shape your understanding about the truth and where it originates?

   _____

   _____

2. According to John 8:31–32, how can we know the truth?

   _____

   _____

3. According to Galatians 4:3, what will the truth set us free from?

   _____

   _____

4. The Bible describes the relationship between Jesus and the truth. Read John 1:17, John 14:6, and John 18:37. How do these verses describe the truth and how we can know it?

   _____

   _____

   _____

5. In John 16:12–13, read about the relationship between the Holy Spirit and the truth. What do these verses further reveal about truth and how we can know it?

   _____

   _____

6. Many people doubt that absolute truth exists or can be known, because varying peoples and cultures understand the truth differently. Pontius Pilate reflected this skeptical view in his conversation with Jesus when he asked, "What is truth?" (John 18:38). Based on what you have studied so far, how does Scripture differ from this skeptical view?

   _____

   _____

   _____

   _____

7. The Bible clearly teaches that absolute truth exists and that it is the same for all peoples and cultures—whether they believe it or not! Read Romans 1:18–20; Romans 2:14–15; John 1:1–3, 14; and 2 Timothy 3:16–17. How can people everywhere know the truth?

   _____

   _____

   _____

8. Read Psalm 119:30, Proverbs 23:23, and Zechariah 8:19. How does the Bible instruct us to respond to the truth?

   _____

   _____

9. According to Acts 17:10–12, how can we know if an idea or teaching is "true" or a lie/false?

   _____

   _____

10. Write a summary statement about what you've learned about biblical truth.

   _____

   _____

   _____

   _____

KEY POINTS TO REMEMBER
The Impact of Worldviews

1. In every society, a dominant worldview informs the majority of its people and how they live.
2. Worldviews spread geographically around the world and penetrate deep into the fabric of society. They also spread through time from one generation to the next.
3. As worldviews spread across the globe and through time, they change and evolve.
4. The Bible teaches that there is only one true worldview.
5. As we "put on" a biblical worldview, we see the world and our lives as they truly are.
6. When we believe and follow the biblical worldview, our lives bear healthy fruit.
7. Only the biblical worldview leads to freedom, maturity, health, and life.

CLOSING THOUGHTS
Exchanging Lies for the Truth

Every Christian engages in a lifelong process of identifying and putting off false elements of his or her worldview and putting on God's view of the world—the biblical worldview. This renewal of the mind is central to the process of sanctification. The "putting off" and "putting on" process requires us to gain deeper understanding of, and live increasingly more consistently with, the biblical worldview.

It is only to the degree that individuals or societies put off false worldviews and put on God's view of the world that they experience life, freedom, and healing as God intends. False worldviews lead to bondage, impoverishment, corruption, and ultimately death.

There can be nothing more important for the Christian believer than the great quest to abandon falsehood and believe the truth. Yet we constantly battle false worldviews and the distortions of God's truth that they represent. Falsehood vies for authority in our lives. The quest is not easy.

The first step is to be aware that we wear worldview "glasses" on our minds. The second step is to examine them. Next, we look to God, his Word, and his creation to understand the truth and recognize its distortions.

PERSONAL APPLICATION

How Has Your Culture Influenced You?

Use the questions below to explore how the dominant worldview of your culture has influenced your thinking.

1. Review the worldview categories listed in this session (naturalism, animism, and biblical theism). To what degree have you encountered any (or all) of these worldview categories in your society?

    _____

    _____

    _____

    _____

2. Which worldview has the greatest influence on your society? How is this influence evident in your society's values, religious beliefs, institutions, laws, and/or policies?

    _____

    _____

    _____

    _____

3. Think back to a time when you visited another culture or hosted people from another culture. Did that experience open your eyes to your culture's dominant worldview? If so, what did you learn?

    _____

    _____

    _____

    _____

4. Describe one way in which the dominant worldview of your culture has affected your thinking and behavior, either positively or negatively.

_____

_____

_____

_____

5. What obstacles do you face in trying to live according to the biblical worldview, instead of this dominant worldview? Have you overcome any of these obstacles? If so, how?

_____

_____

_____

_____

A PRACTICAL RESPONSE
How Do Others See the World?

Are you familiar with the worldview of each of the primary religious groups in the world? Learning about these major worldviews is interesting and can be helpful when you interact with the many people who live according to them.

If you're part of a small group, arrange for one or more members to research Buddhism, Islam, Judaism, or Hinduism so that each religion is covered. (Add more religions to the list, if you wish.) Report back to the group at the next meeting, sharing the basic underlying beliefs of the religion's followers. After you've all shared your research, as a group compare these spiritual beliefs with Christianity. What is similar? What is different? How would this knowledge help in sharing Christ with these groups?

If you're studying alone, choose a religious system that interests you and learn about it.

The next session: *the biblical understanding of reality*

The Truth about Ultimate Reality

*W*hy? Parents know this as a question frequently asked by children. But even as adults we want to know why things exist, why they operate a certain way, or why certain things happen. "Why?" will eventually lead us to some big questions. Perhaps the biggest question is this: why does the universe exist, and where did it originate? Our answer reveals what we believe about ultimate reality. In turn, what we believe is ultimately "real" dramatically affects how we live every day. The answer flows from our worldview, our view of ultimate reality.

As Christians we find the answer to this question in Genesis 1:1, where we learn that God exists and created the heavens and the earth. However, if we hold to the worldview of naturalism, we answer the question this way: "The cosmos [the physical universe] is all that is or ever was or ever will be."[1] According to naturalism, there is no creator God, nor is there any spiritual world. All that exists is matter (physical particles) and energy. The stars and planets formed by accident, with the process proceeding simply according to the laws of nature. The first living cell formed by happenstance, and from that cell, life evolved into the incredible variety of plant and animal life that exists today, including humans. All this happened purely by chance. According to naturalism, God doesn't exist to give the universe and human life purpose and meaning. Without a creator God, there is no basis for morality. There is no right or wrong. There is no good or evil. There is simply the eternal existence of a meaningless, purposeless universe.

In animistic worldviews, there is no lack of spiritual reality. Everything is spiritual, including the "physical" world. Gods or various spirits exist in physical objects such as rocks and trees. According to animistic beliefs, these gods or spirits are often seen as unpredictable and vengeful. People live in fear of them and seek to appease them. People are at the mercy of the gods, unsure from day to day where they stand.

Both naturalism and animism are in direct conflict with the worldview that flows from the pages of the Bible. They are based on destructive lies that eventually lead to hopelessness, fatalism, confusion, and death. Only the biblical worldview, rooted in the existence of an all-powerful, loving, holy, creator God holds the power to transform our lives and societies.

In this session, we'll examine four of these transformational biblical worldview truths: (1) the universe is ultimately personal, (2) the universe is ultimately moral, (3) the universe is ultimately rational, and (4) the universe affirms both unity and diversity.

KEY WORDS TO KNOW
Viewpoints on Reality

Trinity

The Bible consistently teaches that there is only one God, the all-powerful Creator of the universe who must be worshiped and loved exclusively (Deut. 6:4–5; Isa. 44:6). At the same time, the Bible speaks of three persons in the godhead—Father, Son, and Holy Spirit—working together as a team (John 14:26; Rom. 8; Eph. 1:3–14). This doctrine of the three-in-one God is a key distinctive of Christianity and sets it apart from the other major theistic worldviews, Judaism and Islam.

The three persons are not three roles played by one person, nor are they three gods in a cluster. Rather, "he" is also equally "they." The godhead works together, with the Father initiating, the Son complying, and the Spirit executing the will of both.[2]

Moral/Morality

These terms relate to principles of right or wrong thoughts or behavior. The word *morality* may simply speak of persons' adherence to any code of conduct, good or bad, or it may mean adherence to a good standard of behavior. The word *moral* applies to thoughts and actions that are good, *immoral* to those that are evil. God determines the standard for good and evil. It flows from his nature and character as revealed in Scripture. A related word, *amoral,* is also important to understand. It means neither moral nor immoral, as in something's intrinsic character—neither good nor bad. It also is used to describe a person who follows no discernable code of right or wrong behavior. But it is a third sense that Christians need to be aware of. People sometimes use the term *amoral* to designate something supposedly lying outside the sphere to which moral judgments apply. However, God created a *moral* universe, in both senses of the word: God's creation is good, and all of God's creation is a realm in which moral judgments apply.

Righteousness

This term comes from the Latin *rectus,* meaning "straight." It describes a character, or way of being, that is more than ethics or morality (which have to do with behavior). While morality can arise from a person's character, *righteousness* has a transcendent quality. The concept of righteousness expressed by the Old Testament prophets has to do with loving the good, hating evil, and living in obedience to the will of God. *Righteousness* implies a certain consistency within a person. When we speak of the righteousness of God, we are pointing to the basic nature, or character, of his being: he is the ultimate definition of what is good and true, and he has eternal, utterly reliable consistency both within himself and in his relationship with his creation, including us. When we say,

"Jesus was without sin," that is in part a remark on his absolute consistency of character, that he was truly, or *fully*, a righteous man, even though he was born in the flesh and faced all that challenges that we do.

Justice

The word *justice* comes from the Latin *jus*, meaning "right" or "law." It refers to an order, or way of operating, in which each person receives his or her due (what is his or her "right") without depriving others of their due or harming them. This order is based on equity, or fairness and impartiality. It operates consistently according to a structure of laws that applies equally to all and is in place before any particular problem arises.

We call God just for a couple of reasons, each relating to his righteousness and the way reality is defined by his nature. First, God doesn't play favorites; he cares about us all equally, offering closeness with him to all, not just a chosen few (John 3:16). Second, God consistently operates through time according to his own established and universal law of life in his creation. He enables us to learn about this law, through revelation (Exod. 20:12) and his gifts of intellect and conscience. If we do not conform to this law, the consequences are the same for anyone, without privilege.

Evil

Fundamentally, *evil* is the opposite of good. It is also, therefore, in opposition to God, whose nature defines "good." And since God's nature determines the way he has designed his creation and his will for it, to "do evil" is also to act in a way opposite from how he has designed our universe to work—in fact, to "fly in the face of reality." In the end, to do evil is to act against God himself, separating ourselves from him. This is what we mean when we talk about "sin." The logical result of sin is harm to the evildoer, as well as to others, because he or she is trying to operate outside the basic nature of our universe.

Evil that results from the willful actions of free created beings, both angelic and human, is often called *moral evil*. Anything in the natural world that produces pain, distress, loss, or calamity is often called *natural evil.* Diseases, floods, and earthquakes are examples. The causes of natural evil can often be traced back to moral evil. Both humanity and creation lost their original perfection in the Fall because of humankind's evildoing (Gen. 3:17–19; Rom. 8:18–23). In addition, the harm people suffer from natural calamities is often caused or magnified by humanity's violation of God's design for our relationships with each other and the rest of creation.

Because God created us with a degree of freedom to follow or reject him, he created a universe in which evil could exist. Yet he is separate from evil. God hates evil and promises to punish it. His redemptive plan will ultimately triumph over evil.

Laws of Nature

Through observation and experiment, scientists have defined certain principles, or "laws," which describe the particular ways in which physical objects or materials can be expected to behave, or certain phenomena occur, with regularity or uniformity under similar conditions. The law of gravitation, for example, is considered a law of nature because it predictably affects physical objects throughout the universe in mathematically definable ways. God, who created a rational, orderly universe, imposed these laws upon creation.

Rational

Something that is rational conforms to reason and may show orderly, purposeful thought. Human beings are rational creatures because we possess an ability to think about things in an orderly, purposeful way. The universe is rational because it displays signs of reasonableness and purposefulness. The opposite of rational is absurd, irrational, purposeless, or chaotic.

Fatalism

Fatalism is the way of thinking that sees all events or occurrences as preordained, fixed in advance by fate or by God, or the gods, and something one must just accept, having no power to change them.

KEY VERSES TO READ
In the Beginning

In the beginning God created the heavens and the earth.
—Genesis 1:1

1. Who existed before the heavens and the earth?

   _____

   _____

2. What did God do? What does this action reveal about God and his character?

   _____

   _____

   _____

3. Where did the universe originate? How does this information affect your understanding of it?

   _____

   _____

   _____

BIBLICAL INSIGHTS
The Alpha and Omega

The four most important words in the Bible may be, "In the beginning God…" (Gen. 1:1). These first words of Scripture tell us that ultimate reality begins with God and must be seen entirely in relationship to God. "What is God?" asks the *Westminster Shorter Catechism*. It then answers, "God is a Spirit, infinite, eternal, and unchangeable in his being, wisdom, power, holiness, justice, goodness, and truth." In the Bible God describes himself as the "Alpha and the Omega," or the beginning and the end (Rev. 1:8). He existed before the universe was formed. He created it and will exist after it ends.

God created the physical universe by his spoken word (Heb. 11:3). It existed in his mind before he created it. The universe owes its presence to this divine Creator who sustains it moment by moment (Col. 1:17). Ultimate reality is rooted in God's existence. All creation and created beings lead back to him.

Let's look at some life-transforming truths that flow from this incredible reality.

Transforming Truth: The universe is ultimately personal

The Bible teaches that God is not an impersonal, mysterious force or power. Rather he is revealed as a person. The fact that God also reveals himself as the Trinity is important to understand at this point. The Bible describes God as one all-powerful, spiritual being (Deut. 6:4; Isa. 44:6) comprised of three distinct persons—the Father, the Son, and the Holy Spirit (John 14:26; Rom 8; Eph 1:3–14). Within God himself, a loving relationship exists between these three persons (John 14:31; 17:24). Love and relationship are so central to the Trinity, that the apostle John describes God with one word: "love" (1 John 4:8).

God extends this love to his creation, and particularly to humans, whom he made "in his image" (Gen. 1:27). The Creator of the universe loves you. John 3:16 demonstrates this amazing fact: "For God so loved the world that he gave his one and only Son, that whoever believes in him shall not perish but have eternal life." But what does this love look like? The apostle Paul describes it as follows: "Love is patient, love is kind. It does not envy, it does not boast, it is not proud. It is not rude, it is not self-seeking, it is not easily angered, it keeps no record of wrongs. Love does not delight in evil but rejoices with the truth. It always protects, always trusts, always hopes, always perseveres" (1 Cor. 13:4–7).

We observe this love in the person of Jesus and in his sacrificial death on the cross. When we follow his model and sacrificially give ourselves to others with love, we discover what it means to be truly human, to be fully alive (Matt. 16:24–25). God made us to love and be loved. The universe is personal—not impersonal, and at its center, we discover the God of love.

Transforming Truth: The universe is ultimately moral

God is loving, yet Scripture also describes him as perfect (Deut. 32:4), righteous (Isa. 5:16), and holy (Isa. 6:3). Based on these attributes, God created a moral universe where good and evil exist—a universe with absolute, unchanging standards for what is right and wrong. These standards apply to all people and for all time.

God himself defines all that is good. His nature and character establish the standard for what is right, beautiful, and perfect. Evil stems from the rejection of God by morally free creatures—humans and angels. The Bible refers to this rejection as sin, and it is God's nature to hate sin and punish it (Lev. 26:27–28).

In Scripture, God describes himself as "the compassionate and gracious God, slow to anger, abounding in love and faithfulness, maintaining love to thousands, and forgiving wickedness, rebellion and sin." But God also adds that "he does not leave the guilty unpunished; he punishes the children and their children for the sin of the fathers to the third and fourth generation" (Exod. 34:6–7). This punishment relates to God's law. To be true to God's nature, love and law must coexist. Based on his love and his "good, pleasing and perfect" (Rom. 12:2) will for his creation, God's law explains how peoples everywhere should live in a manner that pleases him. This law, a basic summary of which is found in the Ten Commandments (Exod. 20:1–17), is not just for Israel. God's divine law provides the basis for all true and just human laws. God's laws are not arbitrary but flow from his perfect wisdom and love. When individuals and nations live according to these laws, they can experience the life and freedom that God intends for them.

God's law derives from his own moral perfection. Yet as sinful creatures, we are unable to adhere to this perfect standard, and as a result we are subject to God's wrath (Rom. 1:18). We live in a moral universe. Right and wrong exist as eternal standards. Wrong must always be punished. And yet central to God's very moral perfection is his longsuffering love and forgiveness, even for sinful mankind (Exod. 34:6–7a). At the cross, we see these two aspects come together with awesome power and clarity. God's wrath for our failure to adhere to his perfect law is poured out on Jesus, God's own Son, who takes on himself the punishment we deserve.

Christ's death on the cross is God's supreme act of love to each of us. Truly, God is awesome and glorious, deserving of our everlasting devotion.

Transforming Truth: The universe is ultimately rational

Our everyday observations of God's creation reveal an orderly, purposeful universe, governed by natural laws. From the grand vistas of the cosmos to the inner workings of living cells, we discover an intricate design. We do not live in a chaotic universe. Objects do not fly about randomly. Rather, the universe functions with amazing precision.

This principle establishes the foundation for science and discovery. Nicolaus Copernicus, the famous sixteenth-century scientist, knew that the universe was "wrought for us by a supremely good and orderly Creator." As a result, he pursued a better understanding of our solar system, one that would, in the words of theologian Christopher Kaiser, "uphold the regularity, uniformity, and symmetry that befitted the work of God."[3]

According to the apostle Paul, we can understand much about God by observing the wonders and marvels of creation. "For since the creation of the world [God's] invisible qualities—his eternal power and divine nature—*have been clearly seen, being understood from what has been made*" (Rom. 1:20, author's italics). The order and design of creation, revealed through natural laws, is evident. The Bible says this proves the existence of an orderly, rational God who created it all.

Transforming Truth: The universe affirms both unity and diversity

Because God is one being yet three persons, we find a basis for affirming unity and diversity throughout creation. Countless individual parts make up the universe. For example, there are millions of stars and planets. There are various types and amounts of chemical elements. There is a wide variety of life forms—plant, animal, and human. Each part has a unique value yet fits into the universe as a whole.

Or consider human life. There is a wide variety of people from different cultures, speaking different languages. There are two genders, male and female. There is great diversity within the human family, yet the Bible teaches that we spring from the same blood (Acts 17:26) and are made in God's image (Gen. 1:27). The diversity within the human race can be enjoyed and celebrated, yet we cannot forget the ultimate source of our unity and equality.

Other worldviews overemphasize either unity or diversity. Because God himself encompasses unity and diversity, the biblical worldview calls these characteristics into harmony and affirms them both.

DISCOVERY QUESTIONS
Knowing God

God's majesty, beauty, and power are revealed through the pages of Scripture. Open your Bible and read more about the transforming truths of a biblical worldview.

Transforming Truth: The universe is ultimately personal

1. Read John 17:24. What existed before the creation of the universe?

   _____

   _____

2. Read the following verses. What overall theme emerges from them?

   John 14:21 _____

   Romans 8:35–39 _____

   1 John 3:16 _____

   1 John 4:9–10, 19 _____

   Romans 5:8 _____

3. According to the previous verses, how would you describe God's love?

   _____

   _____

4. How has God demonstrated his love toward us?

    _____

    _____

5. Read 1 John 3:16–18. What does God ask of us in response to his love?

    _____

    _____

Transforming Truth: The universe is ultimately moral

6. We often think of love and justice as opposites, yet God reveals him-
    self as both merciful and just. Read Exodus 34:4–7. Why is it impor-
    tant for both attributes to exist within God's nature?

    _____

    _____

    _____

    _____

7. Read the following verses. What do they reveal about God?

    Deuteronomy 32:4 _____

    Isaiah 5:16 _____

    Romans 1:18 _____

    1 John 1:5 _____

8. What incites God to anger? (See Rom. 1:18.)

    _____

    _____

Transforming Truth: The universe is ultimately rational

9. Read Psalm 104:24, Psalm 136:4–9, and Romans 1:20. How do these
    verses describe the universe's order and design?

_____
_____
_____

Transforming Truth: The universe affirms both unity and diversity

10. Read Mark 10:6–9. How is unity and diversity affirmed through marriage?

_____
_____
_____

11. Read 1 Corinthians 12:4–6, 12–13. How can unity and diversity be affirmed in a church?

_____
_____
_____

12. In what other relationships can we affirm biblical unity and diversity? How?

_____
_____
_____
_____
_____

KEY POINTS TO REMEMBER
Ultimate Reality in Review

1. God created everything and is the source of ultimate reality.
2. God is revealed in Scripture as a relational person who extends love to his creation, particularly to humans whom he made in his image.
3. God is perfect, righteous, and holy. Because of this, we live in a moral universe with an absolute, unchanging standard for good and evil. Right and wrong exist.

4. God has created a universe that is orderly, purposeful, and governed by natural laws.
5. God created a universe of both unity and diversity. The biblical worldview affirms both attributes and brings them into harmony.

CLOSING THOUGHTS

Imagine This

According to theologian J. I. Packer, "The highest science, the loftiest speculation, the mightiest philosophy, which can engage the attention of the child of God, is the name, the nature, the person, the work, the doings, and the existence of the great God whom he calls his Father.... It is a subject so vast that all our thoughts are lost in its immensity."[4]

Imagine a society in which the dominant worldview flows from a clear understanding of and love for God. How might this society function? Here are some possible ideas:

◆ People would devote time to prayer. They would realize that a loving and personal God actively works in the lives of people and nations.
◆ Just laws would govern the nation—laws that gain legitimacy from their relationship to God's eternal laws.
◆ Citizens would act with a healthy respect for the law, with even the most powerful citizens made accountable to it.
◆ The society would stand against bribery, corruption, and injustice.
◆ Leaders would exercise power with gentleness and compassion.
◆ All people, including the poor, would receive love and provision.
◆ There would be a deep respect for individuality, diversity, and uniqueness.
◆ There would be an equally strong value of unity and harmony in institutions, from the family to the nation as a whole.

What else might we expect to see in this society?

PERSONAL APPLICATION
What about Your Ultimate Reality?

Psalm 115:3–8 reads, "Our God is in heaven; he does whatever pleases him. But their idols are silver and gold, made by the hands of men.... *Those who make them will be like them, and so will all who trust in them*" (author's italics). The psalm writer says our lives, to a significant degree, will mirror what we believe about ultimate reality.

Use the questions below to think about your own understanding of ultimate reality.

1. In your society, which of the following quotations best describes the dominant view of ultimate reality? Why?

    > Everything that exists came into being at [God's] command and is therefore subject to him, finding its purpose and meaning in him. The implication is that in every topic we investigate, from ethics to economics to ecology, the truth is found only in relationship to God and his revelation.
    >
    > —Charles Colson[5]

    > We exist as material beings in a material world, all of whose phenomena are the consequences of material relations among material entities.
    >
    > —Richard Lewontin[6]

    > God is all, and all is God.
    >
    > —author unknown

2. How does this dominant view affect people's behavior?

_____

_____

_____

3. Are you living more by a biblical understanding of ultimate reality or by the dominant viewpoint of your society? How? Why?

_____

_____

_____

_____

4. What practical changes can you make to live in a manner consistent with the biblical view of ultimate reality? List them, and write a prayer to God, asking him to empower you for these changes.

_____

_____

_____

_____

_____

_____

A PRACTICAL RESPONSE

Investigating Your Culture's View of Reality

This week look for ways that your culture expresses its opinions about the universe and what is ultimately real. Record what you hear, read, and observe through conversations, the media, newspapers, books, and other interactions. Write down, cut out, or make a copy of the answers you discover. Use the five questions below to conduct your research.

◆ Is the universe personal or impersonal?
◆ Is the universe moral or amoral?

◆ Is the universe rational or irrational?
◆ Does the universe reflect unity or chaos?
◆ Does the universe affirm diversity or uniformity?

Share your findings at a future group meeting. Discuss (1) why someone might form a particular view of the universe, (2) how this view compares to the biblical view of reality, and (3) how to relate to someone
who has a particular unbiblical viewpoint.

The next session: *a biblical understanding of humanity*

A Biblical Look at Humanity

The British journalist and essayist Malcolm Muggeridge recalls an interview with Mother Teresa, the famous missionary to the poor of Calcutta, India. Muggeridge posed a question that reflected an opinion of many people in England and around the world: Were there not already too many people in India? Was it worth it to salvage a few abandoned children who might otherwise be expected to die of neglect, malnutrition, or a related illness?

According to Muggeridge, "[It was a question] so remote from her whole way of looking at life that she had difficulty grasping it. The notion that there could in any circumstance be too many children was, to her, as inconceivable as suggesting that there are too many [flowers] in the woods or stars in the sky."[1]

"At the end of life," explained Mother Teresa, "we will not be judged by how many diplomas we have received, how much money we have made, or how many great things we have done. We will be judged by [the words of Jesus], 'I was hungry and you gave me something to eat, I was naked and you clothed me. I was homeless and you took me in' [Mt. 25:35].... [The poor are] Christ in distressing disguise."[2]

All human life, from the moment of conception to the last breath, has immeasurable value and dignity. God created humans in his image, and he deeply loves each individual, whether male or female, rich or poor, and regardless of race, caste, creed, or disability. In every society where this truth penetrates, it initiates dramatic changes, such as the abolition of slavery, improvement in the treatment and status of women and children, care for the unborn and the dying, and service to the poor, broken, and outcast.

When sociologist Rodney Stark wrote about the distinctive characteristics of early Christianity, he concluded that, "above all else, Christianity brought a new conception of humanity to a world saturated with...cruelty and the...love of death. What Christianity gave to its converts was nothing less than their humanity."[3]

Not all worldviews hold this same high view of human life. Naturalism considers people cosmic accidents, products of an evolutionary process whose only purpose is the survival of the species. Because naturalism denies the existence of a spiritual realm, people are physical machines with no spirits or true free will. In the universe there is only one substance—physical matter—and people are made of the same.

A professor in a United States university revealed that his worldview was shaped by naturalism through a question he posed to students: "What is the purpose of the life of an infant who dies of hunger in the developing world?" After a silent pause, the professor answered his own question. "The only purpose for such a life is to become fertilizer for a tree." For the person who holds faithfully to the worldview of naturalism, human life is meaningless and of little value.

In contrast, various forms of animism view men and women as helpless victims of an unpredictable spirit world. In a 1985 trip to rural Ethiopia, Dr. Tetsunao Yamamori, former president of Food for the Hungry International, found a dying infant abandoned alongside a dusty roadway. Alarmed, Yamamori carried the baby into a nearby village, found the mother, and handed the child back to her.

The mother protested, "Put the child back, for she was meant to die." Yamamori countered with the biblical worldview: "The child was not meant to die; she was born to live." He took the infant to a local clinic for medical care.

Both naturalism and animism represent destructive lies that eventually lead to hopelessness, fatalism, and death. Only the biblical view of humanity—the view of Mother Teresa and Dr. Yamamori—holds transformational power.

In this session we'll examine five biblical truths and their power to transform lives and nations. They are: (1) all human life is sacred, (2) all people and nations are of equal value, (3) all people and nations are unique, (4) work is sacred, and (5) humanity is fallen, broken, and sinful.

KEY WORDS TO KNOW
About Human Nature

Sacred

That which is sacred is set apart for service to God or his work. It is consecrated unto him.

Unique

If something is unique, it is without a likeness or an equal. To be unique is to be one of a kind.

Depravity

Depravity means corruption. A corrupt act or practice is "depraved." The fall of Adam and Eve led to the depravity of all humanity. Every part of a human being was corrupted, spoiled, or degraded.

KEY VERSES TO READ
God's Image Bearers

> Then God said, "Let us make man in our image, in our likeness, and let them rule over the fish of the sea and the birds of the air, over the livestock, over all the earth, and over all the creatures that move along the ground."

So God created man in his own image,
    in the image of God he created him;
    male and female he created them.

—Genesis 1:26–27

1. How is humanity different from the rest of creation? How is it the same?

_____

_____

2. What does it mean to be made in God's image?

_____

_____

3. What were people created to do?

_____

_____

4. In creating humanity in his image, God created both male and female. What does this indicate about the value of both?

_____

_____

BIBLICAL INSIGHTS
The Fallen Glory of Humanity

One of the "big questions" asked by people around the world is, "Who am I?" A related question is, "What does it mean to be human?" Naturalism looks to the animal kingdom to find the answer. Why? Because men and women are merely animals, evolved over millions of years from simpler life forms. If we look to the Bible, however, we answer this question in a radically different way. In Scripture we discover that men and women, like nothing else in creation, are patterned after God (Gen. 1:26). When we ask the question, "What does it mean to be human?" we look to God to find the answer. This is one of the most significant, astounding truths in the Bible.

God is spirit (John 4:24) and does not dwell in a body, so bearing his image does not refer to physical resemblances. Rather, we resemble God's nonphysical qualities and abilities. "For instance, God can think, reflect, and choose, and so can we. He is a moral being, and so are we. He is relational, and we likewise."[4] Because we share these attributes with God, we have the capacity for intimate fellowship with him. In fact, he designed us for this relationship. Because God created us in his image, all human life is endowed with inherent worth and dignity. In other words, human life is sacred.

Transforming Truth: All human life is sacred

Human life is created, not evolved. Psalm 139:13–16 beautifully describes this truth:

> For you created my inmost being;
>   you knit me together in my mother's womb.
> I praise you because I am fearfully and wonderfully made;
>   your works are wonderful,
>   I know that full well.
> My frame was not hidden from you
>   when I was made in the secret place.
> When I was woven together in the depths of the earth,
>   your eyes saw my unformed body.
> All the days ordained for me
>   were written in your book
>   before one of them came to be.

God created each of us, and our lives belong to him. He holds each of our days in his hands. He also deeply loves and supremely values each person. Jesus said, "Are not two sparrows sold for a penny? Yet not one of them will fall to the ground apart from the will of your Father. And even the very hairs of your head are all numbered. So don't be afraid; you are worth more than many sparrows" (Matt. 10:29–31).

Because God created individuals, and cares for them so deeply, we realize that human life is sacred. In the words of Malcolm Muggeridge, "this life in us...however low it flickers or fiercely burns, is still a divine flame which no man dare presume to put out, be his motives ever so humane and enlightened."[5] Because life is sacred, it needs to be protected, cared for, and preserved from the moment of conception to the last breath. Even the weakest, most vulnerable, or severely broken human is created by God, cared for by him, and is of immeasurable worth.

Transforming Truth: All people and nations are of equal value

Because all people, regardless of gender or race, are created by God and made in his image, all stand before God equal in value and worth. The 1776 Declaration of Independence crafted by America's founding fathers powerfully and practically expresses this equality: "We hold these truths to be self-evident, that all men are created equal, that they are endowed by their creator with certain unalienable rights, that among these are Life, Liberty, and the pursuit of Happiness." The profound biblical truth about equality counters bigotry, which says, "Because we are different, I am better than you!" Some worldviews actually establish inequality as a virtue. In Hinduism those in the priestly class (the Brahmans) rule all others, while those in the lowest class (the "untouchables") are deemed subhuman. Yet in God's kingdom there are no untouchables, no prejudices that deem one person better than another. All human life is equally valuable, and therefore, all nations are of equal value.

Transforming Truth: All people and nations are unique

While the biblical worldview holds that all people are of equal value, it doesn't mean they share the same personal characteristics. God created each person in a special way, and this uniqueness forms part of his image within us.

Within the Godhead are three persons—the Father, Son, and Holy Spirit—and each fulfills a unique role and function. This unity and diversity within the Godhead resides in humanity as well. All people are equal because God creates them in his image. They all equally share in his nature and attributes. Yet there is also tremendous diversity. There are two genders, male and female. There are differences between cultures and languages, differences in temperament, personality, and gifts. God even gave each of us a unique physical appearance.

This diversity is a part of God's marvelous plan and intention and should be appreciated and celebrated. Appreciating human diversity sets us free to be the special people God created us to be. These twin biblical truths of human equality and human uniqueness and diversity provide a foundation for human community. Diversity without unity leads to chaos and conflict, while unity without diversity leads to stifling conformity and bondage. Only the biblical balance of equality and uniqueness provides a sure foundation on which human communities and societies can be built.

Transforming Truth: Work is sacred

Genesis 2:15 reads, "The LORD God took the man and put him in the Garden of Eden to work it and take care of it." God instructed Adam and Eve to work in the garden and to rule over creation. It's important to note that these instructions occur before the Fall in Genesis 3. God has always intended for us to work. It is not a result of a broken world. Rather, work is a sacred task.

Our God is a creative, working God. His work involved the creation of the universe, and his work continues as he daily sustains it. Because we bear God's image, we are created to work. God has given us hands, minds, and language with which to shape the world. Work is part of what gives us dignity. It allows us to care for our families, our communities, and ourselves. We are to do our work "as working for the Lord" (Col. 3:17, 23–24) in a way that honors and glorifies him.

In fact, the Bible teaches that God has special work—a unique calling—for each of us (Luke 19:11–26; Eph 2:10). He has endowed us with the gifts and "talents" necessary to carry out this calling. This special work represents the part he intends for us to play in his grand redemptive plan for the world. When we understand this, we gain an even deeper appreciation of who we are, how we were created, and the incredible significance of our lives and all human life.

Transforming Truth: Humanity is fallen, broken, and sinful

While the wonderful uniqueness of humanity is true, this does not paint the full picture. Men and women, in their natural, unredeemed condition, stand in rebellion against God.

God created Adam and Eve with the freedom either to obey him or to reject him and suffer the consequences. When faced with this moral freedom, they chose to disobey God by eating of the fruit of the tree of the knowledge of good and evil—something that God had expressly forbidden (Gen. 2:16–17; 3:1–6). From this first act of disobedience sprang all the evil, suffering, corruption, injustice, hunger, poverty, hatred, and violence in the world from that moment forward. The Fall affected not only Adam and Eve but all their human descendants too. The apostle Paul claims, "All have sinned and fall short of the glory of God," (Rom. 3:23) and that "sin entered the world through one man [Adam], and death through sin, and in this way death came to all men, because all sinned (Rom. 5:12).

According to theologian John Stott, "The Fall led to total depravity." Every part of human nature was affected. Yet total depravity "has never meant that every human being is as depraved as he could possibly be, but rather that every part of our humanness, including our mind, has become distorted by the Fall."[6] We still retain the image of God, but it has been distorted. People are still able to love, but now, instead of loving God, many worship idols. People are still creative, but now some use their creativity to plot terrorist attacks.

Only a biblical worldview can explain the existence of evil while at the same time asserting that it is not part of God's intention for creation, thus providing reason to stand against it.

Naturalism denies the existence of evil. It views man in neutral terms, with persons' or groups' violent or other harmful, antisocial, or illegal activities explained as the result of damaging social or economic factors. Based on such false beliefs, men and women throughout history have sought to create perfect societies independent of God and in denial of unregenerate human nature. Such godless attempts can result in even greater evil and bloodshed. Look no further than the Soviet Union under the dictatorship of Josef Stalin (1929–1953) or Cambodia when Pol Pot was prime minister (1976–1979) for evidence.

Animism, on the other hand, accepts the reality of evil, finding its source in evil spirits that cause floods, famine, disease, and death. Yet animism sees evil as an inevitable part of life and fails to stand against it.

Only the biblical worldview provides a clear understanding of the source of evil, as well as a reason to stand against it. According to it, human evil finds its root in fallen human hearts. Only the biblical worldview realistically understands human sinfulness and that our only hope lies in the redemption offered through Jesus. The good news is that God didn't abandon his fallen creation but rather chose to unfold his marvelous history-encompassing plan to redeem, restore, and heal "all things" by means of Christ's blood shed on the cross (Col. 1:20). The gospel holds the power to transform human hearts (2 Cor. 5:17), and from there, real hope exists for social and cultural transformation as well. This transformation is an inside-out process whereby inward heart and mind transformation works its way outward into the social arenas of family and church and ultimately into the various spheres of society such as the arts, business, government, and education. Rather than denying human sinfulness or resigning us to human brokenness, a biblical worldview directs us to God's redemption.

DISCOVERY QUESTIONS
What Is Man?

Open your Bible and read more about the transforming truths of the biblical worldview that shape our understanding of humanity.

Transforming Truth: All human life is sacred

1. Read Psalm 8 and Psalm 139:13–16. How is man (humanity) described in these passages?

   _____

   _____

   _____

2. Read John 3:16–17 and 2 Peter 3:9. What do these passages tell you about the value of every human life?

_____

_____

_____

Transforming Truth: All people and nations are of equal value, yet unique

3. Read Genesis 5:1–2. How was man created? What does this tell you about the equality of all people?

_____

_____

_____

4. Read Acts 17:26–28. What does this tell you about the equality of all nations, and God's desire for the nations?

_____

_____

_____

Transforming Truth: Work is sacred

5. Read Genesis 2:15. Why did God put Adam and Eve in the garden? Is work a curse or a blessing? Explain your answer.

_____

_____

_____

6. Read Proverbs 6:6–11 and 14:23. What can be learned by watching the ants? What is the result of hard work? of laziness?

_____

_____

_____

7. From your own experience, why is work important? What happens when people are denied the opportunity to work?

_____

_____

_____

Transforming Truth: Humanity is fallen, broken, and sinful

8. Read Genesis 6:5–6 and Romans 1:28–32. How wicked is humanity?

_____

_____

_____

9. What was (and is) God's response to sin?

_____

_____

_____

10. Read Isaiah 64:6 and Romans 3:23. Is any person righteous? Describe human righteousness.

_____

_____

_____

11. Read Romans 3:21–24. Do fallen people have hope for redemption? On what basis?

_____

_____

_____

KEY POINTS TO REMEMBER
The Biblical Understanding of Humanity

1. All human life is created by God and endowed with inherent worth and dignity. Human life is sacred.
2. All people and nations (ethnic groups) are equal in value because God creates all in his image.

3. God creates all people and nations (ethnic groups) with unique characteristics, qualities, and roles, and he desires that we respect this diversity.
4. Work is sacred because God works and we are made in his image. He has given us the task of working in his "garden" and caring for it.
5. Men and women, in their natural, unredeemed state, stand in rebellion against God. Yet there is hope for fallen men and women through the redemption offered through Christ.

CLOSING THOUGHTS
Imagine a Society Where...

Imagine a society where the dominant worldview is shaped by a clear understanding of the biblical view of humanity that we've examined in this session. What might we expect?

◆ This society would place a high value on human life, protecting it from conception until death.

◆ Individual human freedom and dignity would be respected, realizing that all people are of equal worth in God's sight.

◆ Human uniqueness and diversity would be celebrated.

◆ People of different ethnicities would live together in harmony.

◆ Men and women would be treated with equal value and dignity.

◆ At the same time, the unique roles and functions of men and women would be respected, appreciated, and celebrated.

◆ Every person would appreciate the value of work and fulfill his or her calling or mission from God.

◆ The system of government would take into account human sinfulness, the thirst for power, and potential for corruption and injustice. In such a system, power would not reside in one individual but be distributed to different "branches" that would act to check and balance each other. That system would make law the king, and all citizens, including the top leaders, would be under its authority.

What else might we expect to see in such a society?

PERSONAL APPLICATION
The People of Your Society

Use the questions below to explore your understanding of humanity and your society.

1. Which of the following quotations best describes the view that the majority of people in your society hold about the meaning of human life? Why?

_____

_____

_____

_____

_____

> The heart of man is not depraved...his passions do not prompt to wrongdoing, and do not therefore...produce evil. Evil flows only from social repression or subversion. [If human beings are allowed] full scope, free play, and perfect and complete development, then universal happiness must be the result.... Create a new form of society in which this shall be possible...then you will have the perfect society.
>
> —Horace Greeley[7]

> Naturalistic evolution has clear consequences.... 1) No gods worth having exist; 2) no life after death exists; 3) no ultimate foundation for ethics exists; 4) no ultimate meaning in life exists; and 5) human free will is nonexistent.
>
> —William Provine[8]

> We human beings have both a unique dignity as creatures made in God's image and a unique depravity as sinners

under his judgment. The former gives us hope; the later places a limit on our expectations.... We can behave like God in whose image we were made, only to descend to the level of beasts. We are able to think, choose, create, love and worship, but also to refuse to think, to choose evil, to destroy, to hate, and to worship ourselves.

—*John Stott*[9]

Religion in its highest form has nothing to do with serving or worshipping God.... Religion in its highest form has to do with serving and worshipping ourselves, and all humankind.... When we return to the dictionary we find that worship is defined as "reverence offered a divine being." Are we not divine beings?

—*Neale Donald Walsch*[10]

2. How does this dominant viewpoint affect behavior in your society?

_____

_____

_____

3. How does this dominant viewpoint affect the meaning and purpose of human life in your society?

_____

_____

_____

4. What is the dominant view in your society about the equality of ethnic groups? How does it compare to the biblical view? For example, how are ethnic minorities treated?

_____

_____

_____

_____

5. How are women, the young, and the aged treated in your society?

6. Are the unique natures and roles of men and women (boys and girls) respected and celebrated? Explain.

7. What is the dominant view of work in your society? How does it affect the workplace and personal lives?

8. What is the dominant view of the human condition in your society? What are some of the consequences of this view?

A PRACTICAL RESPONSE

Investigating Your Culture's View of Humanity

This week conduct similar research to last week's practical response, but look for ways that your culture expresses its beliefs about human life. Record what you hear, read, and observe through conversations, the media, newspapers, books, and other interactions. Write down, cut out, or make a copy of the answers you discover. Use the five questions below to conduct your research.

- ◆ What is the value of life?
- ◆ Is there equality among people and nations?
- ◆ Are people and nations unique?
- ◆ What is the value of work?
- ◆ Is humanity basically good or sinful?

Share your findings at a future group meeting. Discuss (1) why someone might form a particular view of humanity, (2) how this view compares to biblical reality, and (3) how to relate to someone who has a particular unbiblical viewpoint.

The next session: *the biblical understanding of creation*

The Glory of Creation

In his youth George Washington Carver appeared to be headed for failure. He was born to slaves around 1864 on a plantation in Missouri. His father died in an accident shortly before his birth, and slave raiders kidnapped and killed his mother. Yet despite growing up as an orphan among "the poorest of the poor," Carver became a great educator and one of the greatest agricultural researchers the world has ever seen.[1]

Plants interested Carver at an early age. A devout Christian, he had memorized Genesis 1:29, "Behold, I have given you every herb yielding seed; to you it shall be for food" (KJV). Commenting on this verse, he wrote, "'Behold' means to look, search, find out.… That to me is the most wonderful thing in life."[2] For him, "nature in its varied forms is the little windows through which God permits [us] to commune with him, and to see much of his glory, by simply lifting the curtain and looking in. I love to think of nature as wireless telegraph stations through which God speaks to us every day, every hour, and every moment of our lives."[3]

Carver approached God's creation with a mind-set rooted in biblical truth. Nature was a book that revealed the Creator, along with the design and purpose within his creation. Consequently, when Carver discovered the purpose of something in nature, he worked to put it to practical use.

When asked by an agricultural journalist what prompted him to study peanuts, Carver responded:

> Why, I just took a handful of peanuts and looked at them. "Great Creator," I said, "why did you make the peanut? Why?" With such knowledge as I had of chemistry and physics, I set to work to take the peanut apart. I separated the water, the fats, the oils, the gums, the resins, sugars, starches…amino and amedo acids. There! I had the parts of the peanut all spread out before me. Then I merely went on to try different combinations of those parts, under different conditions of temperature, pressure, and so forth. The result was…these 202 different products, all made from peanuts!"[4]

Carver's work eventually resulted in the creation of 325 products from peanuts, more than one hundred products from sweet potatoes, and hundreds more from a dozen other plants common to the southern United States. For Carver, the transforming truths of a biblical worldview opened the door to amazing discoveries.

Unfortunately, other major worldviews don't see the universe as designed by a brilliant Creator. Naturalism assumes the physical universe exists by itself. There is no design or purpose in nature because there is no designer. The appearance of design is merely an illusion. On the other hand, animism views the physical world as a dwelling place for spirits. To cultivate the earth, people first need to negotiate with and appease the gods. Even today, a well-meaning missionary might start to dig a well during a drought, but be stopped by somebody because she would be "disturbing the spirits in the ground."

Our worldview affects our relationship to creation, so in this session we'll examine three biblical truths about creation: (1) creation is an "open system" where resources can be discovered and abundance created, (2) men and women hold dominion over nature, and (3) as God's appointed stewards over nature, we enjoy it, care for it, and preserve it.

KEY WORDS TO KNOW
Our Relationship to Nature

Dominion

The Hebrew word for dominion, *radah*, means reign or rule. To exercise dominion is to hold sovereign authority, governing power, or ultimate control over a defined realm or territory.

Nature

In this session the words *creation* and *nature* can be used interchangeably. They both describe the whole of God's creation, which encompasses both the spiritual and physical realms, including the universe, the earth, and all of its parts. The word *nature* is not to be confused with the worldview of naturalism, which believes in an uncreated or evolutionary physical realm without a spiritual counterpart.

Stewardship

A steward is an employee in a large household who oversees the owner's domestic concerns, such as managing servants, collecting rent, and keeping accounts. Stewardship refers to the duties and obligations of a steward.

Stewardship also describes the responsibility that humans fulfill toward nature. God has ultimate dominion over his creation, but he appointed men and women to carefully manage, care for, and preserve it on his behalf (Gen. 1:26–28; 2:15).

KEY VERSES TO READ
The Biblical Mandate

God blessed [Adam and Eve] and said to them, "Be fruitful and increase in number; fill the earth and subdue it. Rule over the fish of the sea and the birds of the air and over every living creature that moves on the ground."

Then God said, "I give you every seed-bearing plant on the face of the whole earth and every tree that has fruit with seed in it. They will be yours for food. And to all the beasts of the earth and all the birds of the air and all the creatures that move on the ground—everything that has the breath of life in it—I give every green plant for food." And it was so.

God saw all that he had made, and it was very good.

—*Genesis 1:28–31*

1. How did God bless the first humans, Adam and Eve?

_____

_____

2. What did God command Adam and Eve to do? List the tasks.

_____

_____

3. What did God give to Adam and Eve from the earth? Why?

_____

_____

4. How did God describe what he made? Why is this significant?

_____

_____

BIBLICAL INSIGHTS
God's Magnificent Design

From the vast array of the heavens to the glory of a sunset, from the delicacy of a summer daisy to the miracle of a newborn infant, we marvel at the precision and splendor of creation. God created the universe by his spoken word (Ps. 33:6–9). He formed it with a purpose in mind, according to a specific design. And all of creation waits for us to unlock its hidden potential.

The design within creation reflects the beauty and order of the Creator's mind. God's creation is a dynamic work of art, full of colors, patterns, textures, sights, sounds, and smells. In creation, art and science meet.

To better understand the universe's design, examine what the Bible says about the transforming truths of creation. These truths can profoundly change individuals and their societies.

Transforming Truth: Creation is an open system where resources can be discovered and abundance created

According to naturalism, the universe is a giant machine with millions of parts, all working in cause-and-effect relationships. Some describe this view of nature as a "closed system." The physical realm is all that exists. There is no spiritual realm, no Creator. Nature functions without design or purpose, operating according to laws of nature. There can be no interruption or alteration of that function by any outside, or "supernatural," force. Men and women are nothing more than parts trapped in a vast, cosmic machine.

But according to the biblical worldview, the physical universe is part of creation, and that creation is an open system. God, who is spirit (John 4:24), created both the physical *and* spiritual realms. The two realms are distinct but closely interrelated. Because the spiritual realm exists, nature is open to intervention by God, angels, demons, and humans. People are physical and spiritual beings made in God's image. As a result, men and women possess the unique ability to shape creation and culture—to take the things of God's creation and use them in innovative ways. Out of the raw materials in God's creation, they can make new creations. They create literature from common words, music from common sounds, and computer chips from common sand (silicon).

George Washington Carver exemplified the human ability to dream, invent, and create (see introduction). He broke the peanut into its smallest elements and recombined them to create new and useful products. A century later, author and scholar Michael Novak captured this spirit of human innovation: "Countless parts of God's creation lay fallow for millennia until human intelligence saw value in it. Many of the things we describe as resources were not known to be resources a hundred years ago."[5]

God implanted within his marvelous creation the potential for growth and abundance. We find this potential in the miracle of a small seed. Genesis 1:11–12 records that on the third day of creation, God said, "Let the land produce vegetation: seed-bearing plants and trees on the land that bear fruit with seed in it, according to their various kinds." Seeds allow life to reproduce and expand.

Because seeds are so common, we probably take this reproduction process for granted. But imagine a system in which a plant grows only a single piece of fruit, and within that fruit is but a single seed. This system would allow for reproduction but not growth or abundance. Thankfully, this is not the system that God created. Instead, a single seed grows a plant bearing an abundance of fruit, and in many cases, each fruit shelters many seeds! A Kenyan proverb illustrates this glorious system: "You can count the number of seeds in a mango, but you cannot count the number of mangoes in a seed."

Within this system God commanded Adam and Eve to "be fruitful and increase in number; fill the earth" (Gen. 1:28). God desires growth and abundance in his creation. His will is "for the earth [to] be filled with the knowledge of the glory of the LORD, as the waters cover the sea" (Hab. 2:14). His amazing creation is dynamic, with a built-in potential to fill the earth.

Transforming Truth: Men and women hold dominion over nature

In Genesis 1:28, God commanded Adam and Eve to "rule over the fish of the sea and the birds of the air and over every living creature that moves on the ground." Under the authority of God's supreme dominion, men and women rule over creation. We are to exercise dominion over nature and not be dominated by it. We are to harness nature for the benefit of humanity and fight against ravages such as drought, disease, and famine.

According to animism, people can't affect nature. Nature houses the spirits who control the affairs of men and women. People trapped in an animistic worldview can only hope to live in harmony with the rest of creation and attempt to survive. They do not fight diseases and famines but consider them hardships to passively endure. This fatalistic mind-set leads to hopelessness and poverty.

In contrast, God's transforming truth about creation can make a difference in the world. Arturo Cuba, a young Peruvian pastor and missionary, worked with the poverty-stricken Pokomchi Indians in rural Guatemala. Primarily subsistence farmers, they lacked the proper storage facilities for their harvested crops. They'd harvest plenty of corn, but rats ate it before they could adequately feed their children.

Arturo asked the farmers, "Who is smarter, you or the rats?"

The farmers laughed and said, "The rats."

"Do you have dominion over the rats, or do the rats have dominion over you?" The farmers reluctantly acknowledged that in a sense, the rats had dominion over them and their families.

Arturo then taught them the transforming truth that men and women are unique in God's creation. Only they were created in God's image and given the mandate to exercise dominion over the rest of creation. He pointed out that God had blessed them with intelligence and creativity. With a proper understanding of their role to subdue and care for creation, they could overcome the storage problem.

This prompted the farmers to develop a simple, elevated corncrib storage system that protected their harvest from rats. The food supply increased, as did the overall health of the community's children. The idea for the corncribs wasn't imported from another community or country. The Pokomchi developed it, once they understood the transforming truth that people hold dominion over nature.

Transforming Truth: As God's appointed stewards over nature, we are to enjoy it, care for it, and preserve it

When God granted men and women dominion over nature, he also handed them the responsibility to serve and care for it. In Scripture, responsibility, sacrificial service, and care always accompany authority. Jesus Christ himself models this. He has ultimate authority over all creation (Matt. 28:18), yet he exercises his authority by sacrificially serving those under his authority (Mark 10:45).

Genesis 2:15 states, "The LORD God took the man and put him in the Garden of Eden to *work it* and *take care of it*" (author's italics). The word *work* indicates progress. Adam and Eve were to expand the Garden of Eden. God gave Adam and Eve the "tools" for the job, including seed-producing plants, the human ability to produce multiple offspring, and the faculty of human creativity. With these tools, God gave them the mandate to "fill the earth" (Gen. 1:28). Yet while Adam and Eve were to fill the earth and use it for their benefit (Ps. 104:10–15), they were also to care for it. They were to protect, conserve, and tenderly care for the Garden—to keep it healthy, growing, and thriving.

Naturalism's View   *Animism's View*   *Theism's View*

As inhabitants of the earth, we live in God's garden. Yet he entrusts us with the responsibility of stewardship over nature—to work it and to take care of the air, water, soil, plants, animals, or anything else in creation.

We are free to responsibly use creation for our benefit, but as we do so, we must cherish and care for it. Other worldviews emphasize working, but not caring for the environment, which results in its abuse and destruction. Still others focus on caring for the environment, but not working it, which leads to poverty and underdevelopment. The biblical worldview provides the marvelous balance between working and caring. We are God's caretakers, stewards over his wonderful creation. We have a mandate to care for nature!

DISCOVERY QUESTIONS
Caring for Creation

Open your Bible and read more about the three transforming truths about creation.

Transforming Truth: Creation is an open system where resources can be discovered and abundance created

1. Read Genesis 1:3, 6, 9; Psalms 33:6–9; and Hebrews 11:3. How did God create?

   _____

   _____

2. Consulting the same verses, how is God's means of creation different from the way men and women create? How is it similar?

   _____

   _____

3. According to Hebrews 11:3, where does the "visible" originate from? This verse refers to God's creative work, but how could it reflect the creative work of men and women, too?

   _____

   _____

4. Read Proverbs 25:2. Write down an example of something God has hidden that men and women have searched out and discovered.

   _____

   _____

5. In your own words, why would this "hiding" and "searching out" bring glory to both God and humans?

   _____

   _____

6. At the end of his creative activity in Genesis 1:1–27, what did God intend to happen to the earth? What evidence can support your answer?

_____

_____

_____

_____

7. Read Genesis 1:20–22, 27–28; 8:15–17; 9:1. What does God want the earth to be filled with?

_____

_____

_____

8. Why would God want his creation to "be fruitful and multiply"? See Habakkuk 2:14 and Romans 1:20.

_____

_____

_____

Transforming Truth: Men and women hold dominion over nature

9. Read Psalm 8. What is man's relationship to the "works of God's hands"? to nature? Explain your answers.

_____

_____

_____

_____

10. Read Genesis 2:19–20. What does God's allowing Adam to name the animals tell us about God? about Adam?

_____

_____

_____

_____

Transforming Truth: As God's appointed stewards over nature, we enjoy it, care for it, and preserve it

11. Read Genesis 2:15. What did God put Adam and Eve in the garden to do?

_____

_____

12. In Mark 10:42–45 Jesus explains that sacrificial service accompanies true authority. How does this understanding of authority apply to the authority that God has given people over nature?

_____

_____

_____

13. Read Exodus 23:10–11. What did God command his chosen people Israel to do every seventh year? How would this command benefit the land? Who else would benefit and how?

_____

_____

_____

KEY POINTS TO REMEMBER
The Biblical Understanding of Creation

1. God is creator of the physical world. He existed before it did and "spoke" it into existence.
2. God created the natural world to grow and expand, intending his creations to fill the earth. Men and women can also use their creativity to study creation and discover new resources and uses for them.
3. Men and women are commanded to take dominion or authority over nature. They are to responsibly harness nature for the benefit of humanity.
4. This biblical dominion is not domination but stewardship and care. We are to protect, conserve, and cherish nature.

CLOSING THOUGHTS
Imagine a Caring Society

Imagine a society where a biblical view of creation completely shapes the worldview. What might we expect to see?

- This society would value caring for the environment. We wouldn't see garbage, pollution, and smog marring the landscape, air, or waterways.
- People would admire the beauty of creation and how it reflects the beauty of its Creator.
- Well-ordered, productive, sustainable farms would provide for the needs of humanity while pleasing the eye and dealing responsibly with the environment. Their products and methods would be good for people's long-term health.
- Under the guidance of the Holy Spirit, redeemed people would help bring healing to creation (Gen. 1:17; Rom. 8:20–21). Formerly barren wastelands would be brought under responsible cultivation or development, increasing their usefulness and beauty.
- Scientists would develop new and useful resources and technologies to help eliminate poverty, hunger, and disease.
- Through a variety of expressions, artists would rejoice in the beauty, complexity, diversity, and wonder of God's creation and reflect this through their art.

What else might we expect to see in such a society?

PERSONAL APPLICATION
You and the Universe

Psalm 90:2 says, "Before the mountains were born or you brought forth the earth and the world, from everlasting to everlasting you are God." Psalm 24:1 claims, "The earth is the LORD's, and everything in it, the world, and all who live in it."

These passages summarize the biblical understanding of creation. God "brought it forth," and he owns and sustains it. Use the questions below to think about your own and your society's understanding of creation.

1. Which of the following quotations best describes the view your society holds about the natural world? Explain your answer.

    > Knowing that God created the world around us, and ourselves as part of it, is basic to true religion. God is to be praised as Creator, by reason of the marvelous order, variety, and beauty of his works.
    >
    > —*J. I. Packer*[6]

    > We are very much part of the earth…. All of us are, along with the animals, vegetables, minerals, liquids, and gases, a collective planetary being.
    >
    > —*Osiyo Tsaligi Oginalii*[7]

    > [I am] not interested in the utility of a particular species, or free-flowing river, or ecosystem, to mankind. They have intrinsic value, more value to me than another human body, or a billion of them. Human happiness…[is] not as important as a wild and healthy planet…. Until such time as Homo sapiens should decide to rejoin nature, some of us can only hope for the right virus to come along.
    >
    > —*David Graber*[8]

    > The cosmos is all that is or ever was or ever will be.
    >
    > —*Carl Sagan*[9]

2. In what ways does this dominant view of creation affect how people in your society behave?

_____

_____

_____

3. How do you typically think about God's creation? How have your thoughts affected your relationship to it?

    _____

    _____

    _____

4. Based on this session, in what ways might your thinking about creation need to change?

    _____

    _____

    _____

5. What practical things can you do in your everyday life to care for God's creation?

    _____

    _____

    _____

A PRACTICAL RESPONSE

Celebrating God's Creation

Alone or with the group, visit a place that displays God's creation: a forest preserve, public park, botanical garden, body of water, mountain area, or another beautiful location. After walking around and taking in God's glory, have an informal worship time. Read Scripture about God's creation, share what you appreciate about nature, look for ways that God is revealed through creation, sing a few worship songs, and pray. Allow this experience to linger in your mind and spirit in the days to come.

The next session: *the biblical understanding of history*

The Meaning of History

Perhaps it was in a dream. We know that later God spoke to his grandchildren through dreams. Perhaps he was eating breakfast. Perhaps he was alone on some windswept hillside, enjoying a quiet moment. We are not told. What we are told is that sometime in his seventy-fifth year, while he was living a prosperous, seemingly contented life with his wife, Sarai, and his nephew Lot in a place called Haran, Abram heard the voice of God.

God told him to leave Haran—to leave his country, his culture, all that was familiar and comfortable—and go forth to an unknown land and an uncertain future. There is no reason for us to think that he knew where he was being asked to go. The voice simply told him to go.

Then God uttered the mysterious promise that would change Abram's life and human history forever:

> I will make you into a great nation
> and I will bless you;
> I will make your name great,
> and you will be a blessing.

> I will bless those who bless you,
>   and whoever curses you I will curse;
> and all peoples on earth
>   will be blessed through you.

> —*Genesis 12:2*

What made this promise all the more incredible, besides Abram's age, was that he was without children and Sarai was barren. Yet God promised that somehow he would make this old, childless man the father of a great nation—a nation through which all the nations on earth would eventually find blessing.

So Abram went. According to historian Thomas Cahill, these two words, *Abram went*, "are two of the boldest words in all literature." They signal a complete departure from everything that has gone on before—from the beginning of time until that decisive moment. "Out of the human race comes a [man who] has been given an impossible promise...a dream of something new, something better, something yet to happen, something—in the future."[1] The author of Hebrews describes the moment in this way:

> By faith Abraham, when called to go to a place he would later receive as his inheritance, obeyed and went, even though he did not know where he was going.... *For he was looking forward to the city with foundations, whose architect and builder is God.*

> —*Hebrews. 11:8–10 (author's italics)*

The apostle Paul also writes of this moment:

> Against all hope, Abraham in hope believed and so became the father of many nations.... Without weakening in his faith, he faced the fact that his body was as good as dead—since he was about a hundred years old—

> and that Sarah's womb was also dead. Yet he did not
> waver through unbelief regarding the promise of God,
> but was strengthened in his faith and gave glory to God,
> being fully persuaded that God had power to do what he
> had promised"
>
> —Romans 4:18–21

Through Abraham, a new vision of human life and history was unleashed upon the world. A view of history completely different from the animistic views that dominated the world during Abram's time—and which still influence the world today. According to Cahill, Abram's contemporaries "would have laughed [at his] madness.... They would say; a man cannot escape his fate." Cahill writes that the ancient Egyptians would have counseled him to "copy the forefathers [and do what has been done] in the past." The early Greeks would have told him not to "overreach" but "come to resignation." In India he would have been told that time is "black, irrational and merciless. Do not set yourself the task of accomplishing something in time, which is only the dominion of suffering." In China wise men would caution that "there is no purpose in journeys or in any kind of earthly striving; the great thing is to abolish time by escaping...change." The Mayan people in America would have pointed to circular calendars which "repeat the pattern of years with unvarying succession, and would explain that everything that has been comes around again and that each man's fate is fixed. On every continent, in every society, Abram would have been given the same advise...do not journey but sit; compose yourself [and] meditate on the ceaseless and meaningless flow [of time]."[2] But instead, Abram went and history was changed forever.

God called Abram out of this meaningless cycle. He gave him a hope and a destiny. Suddenly life had meaning and purpose. Suddenly, history harbored the potential for progress. Suddenly individual people seemed significant in the larger scheme of things.

In this session we'll examine the biblical understanding of history and explore its transformational power.

KEY WORDS TO KNOW
History Is His Story

Fable

A fable is a brief fictitious tale, often amusing but usually with a moral to the story. Characters are often animals.

History

This English word *history* derives from the Latin word *historia* which is akin to the Greek word *eidenai* and means "to know." History is a chronological record of significant events, often including an explanation of their causes. It also describes a branch of knowledge that records and explains past events.

Linear

Linear means resembling or relating to a straight line. In this session we describe the biblical understanding of history as linear because, like a line, it has a beginning, middle, and end. This view of history contrasts with other worldviews, which consider time to be a constantly repeating cycle of events.

Alpha and Omega

Alpha is the first letter of the Greek alphabet. *Omega* is the last letter of the Greek alphabet.

KEY VERSES TO READ
The Beginning and the End

I saw the Holy City, the New Jerusalem, coming down out of heaven from God, prepared as a bride beautifully dressed for her husband. And I heard a loud voice from the throne saying, "Now the dwelling of God is with men, and he will live with them. They will be his people, and God himself will be with them and be their

God. He will wipe every tear from their eyes. There will be no more death or mourning or crying or pain, for the old order of things has passed away."

He who was seated on the throne said, "I am making everything new!" Then he said, "Write this down, for these words are trustworthy and true."

He said to me: "It is done. I am the Alpha and the Omega, the Beginning and the End."

—*Revelation 21:2–6*

1. Who is the bride in this passage? Who is the "husband?" See also Ephesians 5:25–32 and 2 Corinthians 11:2.

2. What will be different about the New Jerusalem compared to the old or present-day Jerusalem?

3. What is the significance of God referring to himself as the "Alpha and the Omega?"

BIBLICAL INSIGHTS
The Transforming Story

According to scholar James Sire, the Bible reveals history as a "linear, meaningful sequence of events leading to the fulfillment of God's purposes for man."[3] History is linear because it has a beginning, middle, and end. It has a past, present, and future.

Other worldviews have a very different understanding of time and history. Various forms of animism hold to a circular view of time. Everything that has been comes around again. Each person's fate is fixed. There is little hope that the future can be better than the past or present. With little hope for the future, there is little sense of purpose or progress.

Naturalism also has a dark view of the future. Because man has no soul or spirit, he has no hope of life beyond the grave. Life is short and meaningless. The biblical view of history, however, creates expectancy and provides a foundation for progress. Life doesn't have to remain the same. It can be different in the future, even better.

History is meaningful because God is its author. He is the "Alpha and Omega, the Beginning and the End" (Rev. 21:6). He is behind the events of history. The word *remember* appears 166 times in the Bible (NIV). We are commanded to remember what God has done in history and his faithfulness to us. We are to record the great milestones of redemptive history and accurately pass them down to our children and grandchildren (Deut. 4:9–14).

God is the Lord of the past, present, and future. He knows what is happening in the present, and he is intimately involved in guiding and shaping the future according to his purposes and plan. "He changes times and seasons; he sets up kings and deposes them," the prophet Daniel tells us (Dan. 2:21). He is a God who "in all things...works for the good of those who love him, who have been called according to his purpose" (Rom. 8:28). The biblical worldview holds two seemingly contradictory positions in balance. On one hand, the Bible is clear that God is the sovereign author of history and unfolds it according to his eternal plan and purpose. Yet this must not lead to fatalism or apathy on our part. The Bible is also clear that the choices of men and women are significant in shaping history and that God will judge every person based on the choices they make (See Matt. 25:31–46).

Knowing that God is so intimately involved in human history fills us with hope and purpose. We may not understand why certain things occur in our lives, or in history, but we know they are not accidental or purposeless. Our lives have meaning because we are part of "His story." And we know that the God who holds the universe in his hands is a loving, almighty Creator who works in history, redeeming creation from the effects of the Fall.

We can think of the biblical view of history as a story. Not just any story, but a powerful story that can transform individual lives, communities, and entire nations. All stories contain certain key ingredients, including an introduction, a conclusion, chapters or sections, a plot or story line, and characters (usually including a hero and villain). The same is true with the story of history, viewed from a biblical perspective. However, this story is no fable or work of fiction. Rather, it is the true account of human history. This story appears on the pages of Scripture from the opening chapter of Genesis to the final chapter of Revelation. It begins in a garden and ends in a city.

Imagine that this transforming story has twelve "chapters." The first words of chapter one introduce the central and most important character. "In the beginning God created the heavens and earth" (Gen. 1:1). This sentence establishes the foundation and context for the entire story. Animism and naturalism are also stories, but their opening lines lead to stories with dramatically different conclusions. The story of naturalism begins with these openings words, "The Cosmos is all that is or ever was or ever will be."[4]

In chapter one of our story, God creates the physical universe out of nothing. The high point of his creative activity comes with his creation of humans (male and female), made in God's own image. He then places them in the center of a beautiful garden and gives them a task—to be fruitful, multiply, and fill the earth, and to steward and develop God's magnificent creation.

Chapter two of our story tells of the Fall. Here we are introduced to another key character—an evil spiritual being called the serpent or Satan. This evil being enters the garden and deceives Adam and Eve, who fall prey to his lies and eat the forbidden fruit, thus rebelling against their Creator. As a consequence of the Fall, death is introduced into the story—along with hunger, poverty, and all manner of evil. Such things were never part of God's original intention for his creation—they are not "normal." They are, rather, products of man's rebellion against the living God. At this point, it's easy to imagine our story coming to an abrupt end with a rightfully angry God destroying everything that he created. But God, who is described as "compassionate and gracious...slow to anger

[and] abounding in love" (Exod. 34:6) chooses to redeem fallen mankind and the rest of his beloved creation from the bondage of sin and death. The good news is that God didn't choose to abandon his broken creation but chose to redeem and restore it to its original glory. Ours is a story that acknowledges that death, evil, and injustice are real. Their source is the Fall. Yet our story also affirms that there is a loving, almighty God who is engaged in history, redeeming all creation from the effects of the Fall. God's redemptive work in history is the basic plot of the transforming story.

Chapters three through nine narrate God's unfolding strategy to redeem all that was lost in the Fall. God raises up Abraham, and through his descendants, extends his blessing of healing and redemption throughout the world. Israel, the nation birthed through Abraham, Isaac, and Jacob, is central to this process. This chosen nation is selected by God to represent him on earth and serve as a model and messenger of his redeeming love for the nations. The apostle Paul describes Israel this way: "Theirs is the adoption as sons; theirs the divine glory, the covenants, the receiving of the law, the temple worship and the promises. Theirs are the patriarchs, and from them is traced the human ancestry of Christ, who is God over all, forever praised! Amen" (Rom. 9:4–5).

The climax of the story occurs in chapter ten, which describes the life, death, and resurrection of Jesus Christ, the Son of God and the King of the universe. This is the focal point of our story and of all human history. "For God so loved the world that he gave his one and only Son, that whoever believes in him shall not perish but have eternal life. For God did not send his Son into the world to condemn the world, but to save the world through him" (John 3:16–17).

Chapter ten is the most important chapter of the entire story, but it is not the only chapter. In "chapter eleven God establishes his church to carry forth his plan of redemption to the nations. In his "Great Commission," Jesus commands his church to "make disciples *of all nations*... teaching them to obey all I have commanded" (Matt. 28:18–20, author's italics). Our lives are part of this story, and we find them here in chapter eleven. This command is our command. God has given us the honor of participating with him in his grand redemptive plan for all creation.

The dramatic conclusion of our story occurs in chapter twelve. In this chapter Jesus, the King, returns with his kingdom. When he does, all humanity will see him. He will judge all peoples, evil will be punished, and creation will be restored to its original glory. In this final chapter, we read of the new Jerusalem:

> I saw the Holy City, the new Jerusalem, coming down out of heaven from God, prepared as a bride beautifully dressed for her husband. And I heard a loud voice from the throne saying, 'Now the dwelling of God is with men, and he will live with them. They will be his people, and God himself will be with them and be their God. He will wipe every tear from their eyes. There will be no more death or mourning or crying or pain, for the old order of things has passed away.
>
> —*Revelation 21:2–4*

What a marvelous vision! It sounds almost too good to be true. Yet this is no fable. It's a *true* story—it is *the* true story. It is a story that brings hope and purpose—a story that the nations are literally dying to hear. This is the biblical understanding of history.

The nations of this world are waiting for us, the children of God, to take this *entire* story to them as we "teach them to obey all that [Jesus has] commanded" (Matt. 28:20). Unfortunately, many Christians today have neglected to tell the entire story to the nations. In many cases, the church has taken the central chapter of the story—"chapter ten"—and removed it from the remaining chapters of the story. We have held up the gospel—the salvation message of faith in the finished work of Christ—and said, "This is it! This and this alone is our entire story. This is all that needs to be said!"

The problem, of course, is that when the gospel is removed from the rest of our story, those who hear it naturally attempt to insert it into whatever their existing cultural story might be—even if theirs is an animistic or naturalistic story. It is absolutely essential that the church share the gospel of Jesus Christ within its only proper context—the entire story of God's revelation in Scripture. It is only in the context of this story that the gospel makes sense. Our entire story is essential for the transformation of nations.

A construction analogy may be helpful here. Many in the church today have forgotten to lay a foundation for God's people. The gospel is the cornerstone of the foundation, but it is not the whole foundation. The foundation cannot stand without the cornerstone, but the cornerstone is not sufficient to support a whole building. This foundation must be the whole transforming story that we have just summarized.

What is the false, shaky foundation that leads to the death and destruction of people and nations? That foundation is lies! A worldview not founded on reality is founded on lies. Scripture tells us that Satan is the "father of lies" (John 8:44). By spreading his lies, he destroys individuals, communities, and nations. How do we counter his lies? We clothe ourselves in the truth. We, as Christians, have a powerful story that opposes these distorted stories and their fundamentally different understandings of reality, a story that brings hope and healing to the nations.

DISCOVERY QUESTIONS
Our Place in His Story

The power of a biblical view of history becomes more meaningful when you study the Scriptures yourself. Open your Bible and read more about this important transforming truth.

1. Read Genesis 12:1–3. What did God promise Abraham? What did he promise to do through his descendants?

   _____

   _____

   _____

   _____

2. Read Revelation 7:9–17. How do these verses describe the fulfillment of God's promise to Abraham?

_____

_____

_____

3. How do the two previous passages, the first occurring some four thousand years ago and the second occurring in the future, shape the biblical understanding of history?

    _____

    _____

    _____

    _____

4. Did Abraham see God's promise fulfilled in his lifetime? What lesson can we learn for our lives?

    _____

    _____

    _____

    _____

5. According to Hebrews 11:16, what is the reward that God gives to those who, like Abraham, step out in faith and trust in God's promises?

    _____

    _____

    _____

6. Read 2 Corinthians 4:16–18, Philippians 3:12–14, and Hebrews 12:1–3. Based on the examples set by Jesus, the apostle Paul, and others, what should our perspective of time/history be as Christians? What should drive us forward?

    _____

    _____

    _____

    _____

7. Read Job 19:25–27, Matthew 16:27, and 2 Peter 3:10–14. How should the reality of Christ's certain return affect our lives?

_____

_____

_____

8. Read Luke 19:11–26. According to this parable, who is the master? Who are the servants?

_____

_____

9. In the same parable, what do the *minas* or talents represent? What does the master want the servants to do with the talents he has given them? When the King returns, what is he going to ask his servants?

_____

_____

_____

10. Based on this parable, how does God want us to live?

_____

_____

_____

11. Review the story of Joseph's interpretation of Pharaoh's dream in Genesis 41. What was the meaning of Pharaoh's dream (vss. 15–31)? What had God "firmly decided" to do in verse 32?

_____

_____

_____

12. How did Joseph respond (vss. 33–37)?

_____

_____

_____

13. How did Joseph's decision impact the world (vss. 56–57)? What does this story teach about God's control over the events of history and how we should live in response?

_____

_____

_____

_____

14. Read Ecclesiastes 9:13–16 and Jeremiah 5:1. How many people did God require to save each city? What insights do these verses provide about how God uses people to unfold his plan and advance his kingdom?

_____

_____

_____

_____

KEY POINTS TO REMEMBER
A Biblical Understanding of History

1. God is the author of history, so it has meaning and purpose. History is going somewhere!
2. History is a linear, meaningful sequence of events leading to the fulfillment of God's purposes for humanity and creation.
3. Each human has astounding significance because God uses individuals to unfold his history-encompassing redemptive plan. He has given each person unique talents and gifts for this very purpose.
4. The Bible is the record of God's unfolding redemptive work in history. As people understand this true story and their place within it, they are transformed. The same is true for entire cultures.
5. As Christians, we can tell our whole story to the world, not just the gospel. Our story provides the necessary context for the good news of Jesus Christ.

CLOSING THOUGHTS
Imagine This Society

Imagine a society that believes in the biblical view of history that we've examined in this session. What might we expect to see?

◆ People's lives would be infused with purpose and significance because they understand their important part in history.

◆ Citizens would place a high value on human life because each person would be seen as having a significant role to play in God's plan.

◆ We might expect spiritually and relationally healthy churches that understand their central role in God's redemptive plan. Churches would gain great respect within the society as they reach out to serve communities, both in word and deed.

◆ There would be a profound hope for a better future. This hope would foster risk-taking, long-term investment, savings, and planned development.

What else might we expect to see in such a society?

PERSONAL APPLICATION
What's Your Understanding of History?

The biblical view of history is "the transforming story." It holds the power to transform individual lives and entire nations. Use these questions to apply this lesson's principles to your life.

1. Which of the following quotations do you think best describes the view that the majority of people in your society hold about the meaning and purpose of history? Explain your answer.

    History is a story written by the finger of God.
    —C. S. Lewis[5]

    Life is just one damned thing after another.
    —Elbert Hubbard[6]

> Everything an Indian does is in a circle, and that is
> because the Power of the World always works in circles.
> … Even the seasons form a great circle in their changing,
> and always come back again to where they were. The life
> of a man is a circle from childhood to childhood, and so
> it is in everything where power moves.
>
> —*Black Elk*[7]

_____

_____

_____

2. What are some of the consequences of this dominant view? How
    does it influence how people behave in your society?

_____

_____

_____

3. What's your own personal understanding of history?

_____

_____

_____

4. Are you living as someone who knows that the sovereign God's
    redemptive plan for creation is marching forward and will be suc-
    cessful? Why, or why not? Consider the specific role that God has
    given you within his plan.

_____

_____

_____

5. Read 2 Peter 3:10–18 again. What practical changes do you need to
    make in your life to live in the manner that the apostle Peter
    describes? Describe two or three changes, and share them with a
    friend who can hold you accountable.

_____

_____

_____

_____

_____

A PRACTICAL RESPONSE
Reenvisioning History

Use the following activities to reflect on how God's truth could have influenced the past and how it still might influence the present and future. Complete one or all of the following activities by writing out your responses or discussing them as a group. Alternatively, split into three smaller groups, each completing a different exercise, and report your ideas to the larger group. Be creative in your storytelling!

1. Choose a story from the Bible in which people disobeyed God's commands and suffered disastrous results. Rewrite the story as if the people had followed God's instructions. What would they say and do? How would the story end? How would history have been altered? Remember that people are flawed, so they do not have to behave perfectly. Yet help them somehow follow God's will.
2. Select a story from your country's history and rewrite it according to the same parameters explained in exercise 1.
3. Identify a current situation in your country and create a progression and ending that is influenced by one person's obedience to God. How would acknowledging God's truth and redemptive purpose influence the future?

Members of your group may not agree about what it means to follow God's laws in certain situations, so consider creating more than one scenario and discussing them together.

The next session: *how the enemy targets a culture*

The ABCs of Culture

The town of Constanza lies in a fertile valley surrounded by picturesque mountains in the Caribbean nation of the Dominican Republic. Water is plentiful there, and the climate stays moderate year-round. On the floor of the valley, several Dominican families eke out a living by working their small, subsistence farms. They are some of the poorest people in the nation.

At the same time, large homes and villas overlook the valley, each with a spectacular view of the countryside. Japanese immigrants, who moved to the Dominican Republic shortly after World War II, own the houses. They left Japan as impoverished immigrants with virtually nothing but the clothes on their backs. Like the local farmers who work on the valley floor, they also labored as poor farmers after their arrival. Yet after a few decades, they became prosperous, while native farmers continued to struggle with poverty in the midst of this breathtaking setting.

What accounts for the difference between these two groups? They shared identical physical circumstances and natural resources. The probable answer resides in their different worldviews.

The Japanese settlers brought with them a set of ideas that value hard work and perseverance in the face of difficulty. Japanese parents trained their children never to give up. The local Dominican farmers, on the other hand, held to a fatalistic belief system. For them, poverty was a given. They were poor because their fathers before them were poor, as were their grandfathers; poverty was just their destiny, their lot in life. Such fatalism made them passive in the face of hardships, believing that "whatever will be, will be."

However, destructive beliefs were not unique to the Dominican farmers. In fact, a different but equally destructive set of beliefs led to the Japanese immigration in the first place. A deep-seated sense of racial superiority fueled Japan's aggressive colonization of East Asia, beginning in 1895 and culminating with their invasion of China in 1936 and progressive movement into Southeast Asia. This and their pact with the Nazis in Europe led to their involvement in World War II. This war wreaked destruction upon Japan and led directly to the immigration of the Japanese farmers.

All nations, to some degree, hold to destructive, false beliefs, even nations where the church is active and prosperous. Churches abound in the United States, and a Christian subculture of books, television, and movies is prevalent. Nine out of ten adult Americans profess belief in God and own at least one Bible.[1] Yet between 1973 and 2001, thirty-eight million babies were killed through abortion[2] and the rate of divorce among Christians and non-Christians is essentially the same.[3]

How can such things happen in a "Christian" nation? A poll taken by the Barna Research Group in January 2000 suggests an answer. It revealed that less than half of all "born-again" Christians in the United States (approximately 44 percent) believed that "absolute moral truth" exists.[4] The majority of American Christians are far from certain about the existence of absolute standards for right and wrong. For most Americans, truth—if it exists at all—is unknowable. Therefore people are left with little or no moral constraints.

These three beliefs—fatalism, racial superiority, and relativism—are rooted in lies. As with all lies, their consequences prove terrible and damaging. Behind all lies stands Satan, the father of lies himself. But because this is God's world, there is hope for those bound by Satan's counterfeits. The truth is more powerful than lies, and God's word is true. Satan is powerful, but God is more powerful still.

In this session we'll examine how Satan distorts God's truth and how this twisted viewpoint results in a variety of destructive consequences. When individuals and cultures believe these distortions, they become enslaved.

KEY WORDS TO KNOW
Ideas Reap Consequences

Consequence

A consequence is an event or situation that results from an act, cause, principle, or set of conditions.

Counterfeit

Something that is counterfeit is made in imitation of what is genuine or superior, especially with the intent to deceive or defraud.

Elementary

The word *elementary* means primary, initial, or rudimentary. It indicates the simplest elements or principles of an idea or thing.

Hedonism

Hedonism is a doctrine or belief that pleasure or happiness is the highest good and thus should be the chief end or purpose of one's life.

Principle

A principle is an accepted rule of conduct or action. The principles in which one believes establish or define one's code of conduct.

KEY VERSES TO READ
The Father of Lies

You belong to your father, the devil, and you want to carry out your father's desire. He was a murderer from the

> beginning, not holding to the truth, for there is no truth
> in him. When he lies, he speaks his native language, for
> he is a liar and the father of lies.
>
> —*John 8:44*

In the verse above, Jesus is addressing a group of Pharisees and other Jews (John 8:13, 22) during his visit to Jerusalem for the Feast of Tabernacles (John 7:2–10).

1. How does Jesus describe Satan in this passage?

    _____

    _____

2. What is central to the work of Satan?

    _____

    _____

3. What is Satan's "native language"?

    _____

    _____

4. What happens when individuals or nations believe Satan's lies? See Galatians 4:9.

    _____

    _____

5. By contrast, how does Jesus describe himself in John 14:6?

    _____

    _____

BIBLICAL INSIGHTS
Enslaving People and Nations

As the apostle Paul describes in Romans 1:18–32, when fallen men and women exchange the truth of God for lies, terrible consequences are the inevitable result. These consequences affect more than individuals as satanic lies penetrate into a nation's culture, corrupting customs, practices, social institutions, structures, and laws. Truth is the foundation for a nation's and a community's healthy development, but lies ensure their destruction.

E. Stanley Jones, a great missionary statesman to India in the past century, once said, "We do not break God's laws, but rather we break ourselves against God's laws."[5]

Satan Enslaves Nations

In the key verse for this session, John 8:44, Jesus describes Satan as the "father of lies." When Satan speaks, it is his nature to lie.

The Bible explains that Satan uses his lies to enslave us. But Satan does not lie just to individuals. His lies enslave entire nations (Rev. 20:3). In this effort, he uses two primary weapons. The first weapon is described in Colossians 2:8 as human-centered philosophy. In this verse, Paul does not attack the study of philosophy. In fact, the word *philosophy* means "love of wisdom," and as Proverbs 3:13 says, "Blessed is the man who finds wisdom." Rather, Paul means that one of Satan's primary tools of enslavement is "philosophy which depends on...the basic principles of this world rather than on Christ" (Col. 2:8).

In the same verse, Paul describes such philosophy as "hollow and deceptive," and "based on human tradition." It passes down from father to son, from one generation to the next. The apostle Peter wrote in a similar vein, "For you know that it was not with perishable things such as silver or gold that you were redeemed from *the empty way of life handed down to you from your forefathers*, but with the precious blood of Christ, a lamb without blemish or defect" (1 Pet. 1:18–19, author's italics).

What are the "basic principles of the world" that the apostle Paul refers to in Colossians 2:8? In Galatians 4:9 he asks, "How is it that you are turning back to those *weak and miserable principles*? Do you wish to be *enslaved* by them all over again?" (author's italics). Paul describes these principles as "weak and miserable." The Greek word for "principles" in this verse is *stoicheia*, which literally means basic, fundamental, or elementary principles.

We encounter basic or elementary principles in our everyday lives. If we want to learn another language, we begin with the fundamental principles of that language—its alphabet and basic rules of word order and perhaps a little grammar—along with a few basic words. If we want to learn mathematics, we first must learn about numbers and what they represent. If we want to draw or paint satisfactory pictures of things, we first must learn a few basics about proportion, perspective, shading, and, if using color, how basic colors combine to create the hues we want. If we want to be able to read music, we need to start with the elementary principles of music notation—what symbols represent what tones and time values.

In the same way, basic principles build the foundation of human cultures. They are the ABCs of culture. Paul refers to these elementary principles when he uses the word *stoicheia*. Satan targets these elementary principles for his deceptive work. He uses false "first principles" to enslave nations.

Gailyn Van Rheenen, a missionary to Kenya in the 1970s, wrote this in his examination of spiritual warfare:

> [T]he *systemic view* [of spiritual warfare] sees the powers as personal spiritual beings who are actively impacting the socioeconomic and political structures of societies. These powers have established their own rules and regulations that pull cultures away from God. The elementary principles [*stoicheia*] spoken of in Pauline writings (Gal. 4:3; Col. 2:8, 20 NASB) are an example of this.... [*Stoicheia*] are illustrated by legalistic observances of the law, worship of angels, and returning to pre-Christian animistic practices. *Stoicheia* within these contexts are the demonic contortions of human society. The powers, although personal spiritual beings, have invaded the very fabric of society. Thus even Christian institutions reflect these demonic influences when the powers invade human institutions.[6]

The Building Blocks

We can think of elementary principles (*stoicheia*) as cultural building blocks. In most—if not all—cultures in the world, some building blocks align with biblical truth. These "kingdom" building blocks support what is moral and beautiful within a society. We find kingdom building blocks in music, art, science, law, technology, and education. It is probable that every culture embraces at least some aspects of biblical truth. Any bit of this truth found within a culture can be nurtured, affirmed, and encouraged.

Also, in all cultures of the world, Satan introduces counterfeit building blocks founded on lies. They are the immoral and profane features in any culture. For example, slavery in the United States was based on the lie that people with white skin are superior to those with black skin. The abuse and subjugation of women in many cultures is based on the lie that men are superior to women. The caste system in India is based on the lie that people from one group are more valuable than those from another group.

These lies, or counterfeit building blocks, exist in every culture. They represent what the apostle Paul refers to as hollow, deceptive, weak, and miserable elementary principles. They are to be exposed, opposed, rooted out, and replaced with kingdom building blocks based on God's eternal, revealed truth.

Although each culture contains both truth and lies, the cultures that have more truth, goodness, and beauty create societies with greater freedom, justice, prosperity, and compassion. The cultures with more falsehood, evil, and ugliness produce societies that prove more callous, enslaved, and corrupt.

Examples of Satanic Counterfeits

Though Satan plants many lies within cultures, these counterfeit beliefs are most prevalent:

Truth does not exist, and therefore, man is not accountable. This lie flourishes in many Western nations influenced by the naturalistic worldview. If there is no God, hedonism and rampant consumerism become the logical approach to life. If we can do whatever we please without fear of ultimate, divine judgment or accountability, and if there is no higher way to dedicate ourselves to, then we should "eat, drink, and be merry, for tomorrow we die." Thus, self-gratification has become one of the highest values of many Western nations.

If truth exists at all, is it unknowable. Naturalism and animism both have distorted understandings about truth. Naturalism allows no room for the notion of transcendent, absolute truth. All that exists is matter and energy in a closed, cause-and-effect universe. Truth is whatever we want it to be. Many animistic cultures also consider truth to be unknowable. Even in one of the world's major religions, Hinduism, the principle of *aviya* means "to worship the gods in ignorance." In this sense, Hindu society actually values ignorance. Imagine that you are a missionary who wants to teach illiterate Hindu people in India how to read, so they can access the Bible in their own language. When you begin to understand Hindu culture, it slowly dawns on you that, in many parts of the Hindu world, if you encourage the poor to learn to read, you are asking them to sin!

Human life is of little value. As a consequence, abortion has become a common practice—and is even cherished as a right—in cultures where naturalism thrives. Few people speak out for the millions of unborn children sacrificed on the altar of "choice." Animism also accords little value to human life. Hinduism, for example, has no rationale for why people in need should be helped. The poor are destined to poverty because of what they did in their past lives. Unlike Christianity, Hinduism does not value individual people or see them as "fearfully and wonderfully made" in the image of God (Ps. 139:14).

Such lies are terrible and destructive. Oh, how the world needs to hear the transforming story that conveys the biblical worldview! For only the biblical worldview reflects the truth—truth that holds transformational power for people and nations trapped in a satanic web of lies.

DISCOVERY QUESTIONS
The Terrible Exchange

Scripture explains the reality and consequences of satanic deception, and offers guidance on what we can do to oppose Satan's lies. Open your Bible and discover these important truths for yourself.

1. Read Romans 1:18–32. Then focus first on verses 18–20. Why is God angry at humanity?

    _____

    _____

    _____

2. What does the word *suppress* imply about humanity's ability to know the truth?

    _____

    _____

    _____

3. What has God revealed to all people through his creation?

    _____

    _____

    _____

4. Focus next on verses 21–24. When people knew about God through his creation, in what ways did they respond? What did this result in?

    _____

    _____

    _____

5. Focus next on verses 28–32. What did the people think was not important? How did this impact their values and behavior?

    _____

    _____

    _____

6. In your opinion, why are ideas, beliefs, and mind-sets important?

    _____

    _____

    _____

    _____

7. Read Ephesians 6:10–12. What is our struggle not against? What is it against?

    _____

    _____

    _____

8. Describe the enemy in your own words.

    _____

    _____

    _____

9. Read John 8:44; Revelation 12:9 and 20:3, 7–8; and 2 Corinthians 4:4. Who is Satan? What does he do? To whom does he lie?

    _____

    _____

    _____

10. What has "the god of this age" done according to 2 Corinthians 4:4?

    _____

    _____

    _____

11. Read Galatians 4:3–10. How does the apostle Paul characterize the believer's past? See verses 3 and 8.

    _____

    _____

    _____

12. What did God do for us in verses 4–5?

    _____

    _____

    _____

13. What are the present consequences for believers? See verse 7.

_____

14. What is the future choice for believers? See verse 9.

_____

15. What does Paul identify as the means or methods by which we were enslaved and may possibly be enslaved again? See verses 3 and 9–10.

_____

16. Read John 8:31–32. How are we set free?

_____

17. According to Ephesians 6:13–18, what can we do to "stand against the devil's schemes"? What is the first item of armor we're to put on?

_____

KEY POINTS TO REMEMBER
The ABCs in Review

1. The Bible describes Satan as "the father of lies."
2. Satan opposes God and, therefore, the Bible and a biblical worldview.
3. Satanic deception affects not only individuals but nations. Satan's lies penetrate customs, practices, institutions, social structures, and laws.

4. The enemy targets the elementary principles of a culture and corrupts them for his destructive purposes.
5. When individuals and nations believe and act on lies, they become broken and enslaved.
6. Only God's truth can bring release, freedom, and healing from lies.

CLOSING THOUGHTS
Breaking Free from Deception

Physical poverty doesn't "just happen." Rather, counterfeit cultural building blocks such as fatalism, prejudice, and pride play an important role in determining whether people suffer from poverty, corruption, or other forms of brokenness. When these satanic lies become part of a culture's foundation, they eventually seep into a society's laws and structures. They end in corruption, injustice, lack of respect for human life, and many other cultural ailments.

Ultimately, brokenness traces back to sin and rebellion against the Creator. When we recognize this in our lives, we cry out with the apostle Paul, "What a wretched man I am! Who will rescue me from this body of death? Thanks be to God—through Jesus Christ our Lord!" (Rom. 7:24–25). How thankful we can be that God's power is stronger than evil, and that he provides a means of rescue from our bondage to sin and satanic deception. His powerful Word of truth makes this possible.

"Therefore…through Christ Jesus the law of the Spirit of life set me free from the law of sin and death. For what the law was powerless to do in that it was weakened by the sinful nature, God did by sending his own Son in the likeness of sinful man to be a sin offering. And so he condemned sin in sinful man, in order that the righteous requirements of the law might be fully met in us, who do not live according to the sinful nature but according to the Spirit" (Rom. 8:1–4).

And "if the Son sets you free," says Jesus, "you will be free indeed" (John 8:36).

PERSONAL APPLICATION

Deceiving the Nations

Revelation 20:1–3 says, "And I saw an angel coming down out of heaven, having the key to the Abyss and holding in his hand a great chain. He seized the dragon, that ancient serpent, who is the devil, or Satan, and bound him for a thousand years. He threw him into the Abyss, and locked and sealed it over him, to keep him from deceiving the nations."

Satan deceives both individuals and nations. Still, his doom is sure, and we can take hope and courage from this fact. Use the questions below to reflect on ways that Satan deceives your nation and how you can stand against his evil work.

1. What ideas or beliefs does Satan use to enslave your culture or nation? These are his counterfeit cultural building blocks. If you can think of several, write them down.

_____

_____

_____

2. Choose one of your answers from the first question—perhaps the one that seems the most destructive to your nation or culture. Do you know the historical roots of this idea in your culture? In other words, where did the idea originate? If you know, write a brief explanation.

_____

_____

_____

3. How is this idea expressed in words, phrases, songs, stories, jokes, laws, practices, or behaviors?

_____

_____

_____

4. What are some of the results from following this idea? What are its consequences for individuals, families, churches, and your nation as a whole?

_____

_____

_____

_____

_____

5. How has this idea affected you personally?

_____

_____

_____

_____

_____

6. If this belief represents a satanic deception or lie, then what is the truth as revealed in Scripture? List specific verses or passages of Scripture, if you know them.

_____

_____

_____

_____

_____

7. Take time to prayerfully consider your answers to the questions above. Have these questions revealed something you need to personally repent from? If so, do that now. You could write out your prayer below.

_____

_____

_____

_____

_____

_____

_____

8. As a member of your society, is there something you could repent of
    on behalf of your nation or culture? (See Isaiah 6:5.) In addition to
    prayer, what is one thing you or your church could do to counter the
    satanic deception you identified in this exercise?

_____

_____

_____

A PRACTICAL RESPONSE
Countering Satan's Lies

Return to the Personal Application section of this session. This section ended by asking you to identify one thing you or your church could
do to counter the satanic deception you described as part of the exercise.
Now make a plan and carry it out. Your plan might include:

◆ A description of the satanic deception and its consequence(s).
◆ A description of a specific thing that you will do to counter the
  deception.
◆ A list of specific steps or tasks involved. For example, a good first
  step would be to begin with prayer.
◆ A list of any resources that are needed and how you'll obtain them.
◆ A list of people involved.
◆ A completion date.
◆ The name of someone with whom you will share the plan and who
  can hold you accountable for carrying it out.

After implementing your plan, do a simple evaluation. What was the
result? What might you do differently next time?

The next session: *putting on the biblical worldview*

~ Putting on the Biblical Worldview

It has been described as "the greatest moral achievement of the British people" and "one of the turning events in the history of the world,"[1] but it almost didn't happen.

In the sixteenth century, when William Wilberforce was twenty-five years old and a young British politician, he experienced a "Great Change." He heard the gospel, responded in faith, and was born again. According to Christian essayist Os Guiness, at first the young man wanted to quit his job in politics and enter full-time ministry as a pastor. "He thought, as millions have thought before and since, that 'spiritual' affairs are far more important than 'secular' affairs such as politics," explains Guiness.[2]

Fortunately, John Newton, the writer of the hymn "Amazing Grace," a pastor and before his conversion to Christianity a slave trader, encouraged Wilberforce to pray carefully about this decision. "It's hoped and believed," Newton wrote to Wilberforce, "that the Lord has raised you up for the good of the nation."[3]

After much prayer and thought, Wilberforce agreed. He changed his mind and remained in politics as a committed, evangelical member of the British parliament. Shortly after this, on Sunday, October 28, 1787, Wilberforce recorded in his journal the vocation that he felt God had given him. "God Almighty has set before me two great objects, the suppression of the Slave Trade and the Reformation of Manners."[4]

"So enormous, so dreadful," he later told the British House of Commons, "so irremediable did the [Slave] Trade's wickedness appear that my own mind was completely made up for Abolition. Let the consequences be what they would, I from this time determined that I would never rest until I had affected its abolition."[5]

And he did not rest. At the time of Wilberforce's conversion and calling, the African slave trade formed a cornerstone of the British economy. Only a few people thought of it as wrong or evil. Powerful vested economic interests viciously opposed Wilberforce, as did a number of British celebrities and most of the royal family. "When Wilberforce presented his first bill to abolish the slave trade in 1791, it was easily defeated 163 votes to 88. But Wilberforce refused to be beaten. With his abolitionist colleagues, he continued to press for the end of the slave trade, and eventually, for the full freedom of all slaves. Wilberforce died on July 29, 1833. One month later Parliament passed the Slavery Abolition Act that gave all slaves in the British Empire their freedom."[6]

The life of William Wilberforce exemplifies how God can use someone committed to the biblical worldview to transform an entire society. Wilberforce understood that biblical truth isn't to be confined to the "spiritual" areas of life. It is to penetrate the marketplace of ideas. Had Wilberforce gone into "full-time Christian service," he may have been a fine pastor but he wouldn't have served as "salt and light" (Matt. 5:13–16) within Parliament, and the abolition of the slave trade may not have happened, or at least not when it did—it was a near miss.

In this session we'll examine how to "put on" the biblical worldview and then live it out in the context of our families, communities, and nations.

KEY WORDS TO KNOW
A Christian Mind

Presupposition

A presupposition is a fact or statement such as a proposition, axiom, or notion that is "presupposed" or taken for granted. It is similar to the word *assumption* defined in session 1.

Vocation

The word *vocation* evolved from the Latin word *voco,* from which the English word *voice* is derived. The original meaning indicated hearing and responding to the voice of God. A vocation was God's summons or call to an area of service. Today the word *vocation* has lost much of this original, spiritual meaning and typically refers to employment, occupation, or a trade.

KEY VERSES TO READ

Renewing Your Mind

> Do not conform any longer to the pattern of this world, but be transformed by the renewing of your mind. Then you will be able to test and approve what God's will is— his good, pleasing and perfect will.

> *— Romans 12:2*

1. What are we to conform to no longer?

2. How are we to be transformed?

3. What will this transformation result in?

BIBLICAL INSIGHTS

Putting It On, Living It Out

From Israel in the Old Testament to the church in the New Testament, the great refrain throughout Scripture is that of Romans 12:2: "Do not conform any longer to the pattern of the world." Though the disciples knew how the world believes and operates, Jesus said it should be "not so" with them (Mark 10:35–42). The apostle Paul echoes this in Ephesians 4:22–24, where he admonishes us to "put off the old self," which is characterized by false beliefs and worldly, destructive behaviors, and to "put on the new self created to be like God."

Of course, being like God means learning to think like him. It means being "transformed by the renewing of your mind" (Rom. 12:2). A transformed mind can naturally lead to a transformation in our behaviors and, ultimately, our entire lives. As British theologian John Stott says, "If we want to live straight, we have to think straight. If we want to think straight, we have to have renewed minds."[7]

This transaction of "putting off" false worldviews and "putting on" the biblical worldview does not happen automatically when we accept Christ as Savior. Nor is the process easy or simple. Rather, it is an ongoing, lifelong process. It is a discipline. Empowered by the Holy Spirit, we learn to consciously discipline ourselves to think and operate according to the biblical worldview and to apply biblical truth in all areas of life, even in the small things. If we do not learn this discipline, by default we will think and operate according to the dominant worldview of our surrounding culture.

To put on biblical truth, we first understand the basic presuppositions of Scripture and then contrast them with the competing presuppositions of our surrounding culture. In short, we learn to think "worldviewishly."

For many Christians, biblical faith influences only a small part of their lives and thoughts. While the truths of Scripture may inform their "spiritual" lives, it may only nominally impact how they think and behave in other parts of their lives, such as their vocations, families, or communities. It is not uncommon for believers to live with two different belief systems—one for their churches and "spiritual lives" and one for the marketplace and their personal lives. Indeed, for nations to be discipled as Christ commanded in Matthew 28:18–20, followers of Christ must "put on" the biblical worldview and then apply its principles to every area of life—not just to the "spiritual" area, but to *every* area. Then they can purposefully take the truth out into the world. They live it out in their families and through their vocations.

As we end this study, consider how to *put on* and *live out* the biblical worldview. This is not an academic exercise. Rather, it is the essence of being "salt and light" in the world (Matt. 5:13–16). For believers there is nothing more important than walking in relationship with God and living according to his revealed truth. When a sufficient number of believers do so, cultures will be transformed and entire nations will be discipled.

Be Transformed!

In Matthew 22:37–38 Jesus summarizes God's intentions for humanity in one simple sentence: "'Love the Lord your God with all your heart and with all your soul and with all your mind.' This is the first and greatest commandment." Most of us know what it means to love God with all of our hearts, but what does it mean to love God with the entire mind?

The apostle Paul helps answer this question. In Romans 12: 2, quoted in the Key Verses to Read section, Paul urges us, "Do not conform any longer to the pattern of this world, but be transformed by the renewing of your mind." It is possible to be "born again" and to engage in "spiritual" activities but still carry a mind-set that conforms to the "pattern of this world." If this seems hard to believe, read Mark 10:35–45 again and look at why Jesus scolded his disciples.

From the time of our natural birth, we are influenced by ideas. We receive these ideas from our parents, friends, teachers, employers, and others. We also pick up ideas from the media and popular culture. Some of these ideas may align with biblical truth, but most do not. When we become children of God, this set of ideas or worldview does not vanish automatically. Rather, we must determine that we will love God with our minds. We must uncover our unconsciously held assumptions and expose them to the light of biblical truth. As we do, we will be transformed by the renewing of our minds. Using even stronger language, the apostle Paul calls us to "demolish arguments and every pretension that sets itself up against the knowledge of God, and...take captive every thought to make it obedient to Christ" (2 Cor. 10:5). All believers are called to engage in this battle.

Putting It On

To renew the mind we must engage in a deliberate process of studying God's Word. We must allow the Word to penetrate every corner of our minds. This may sound like an impossible task. Some argue that we are so thoroughly shaped by our surrounding culture that taking on God's perspective about the truth is virtually impossible. According to this view, we are mentally trapped within our culture, which determines how we view everything, including Scripture.

In one sense, this is true. As Jesus says, "With man this is impossible, but with God all things are possible" (Matt. 19:26). In our own strength and resources, it is impossible to truly understand the truth. But we can comprehend it with God's divine help that is available in three important ways. First, when we are saved, a remarkable transformation occurs (2 Cor. 5:17). It permeates every part of us, including our minds and how we think. Yet we still live in a fallen world and therefore still struggle with false worldviews. Satan still tells us lies, and we are prone to believe his deceptions. Nevertheless, as new creatures in Christ we now possess God-given mental resources to help us comprehend the truth.

Second, God's revealed truth in Scripture is inspired and divinely powerful. It is equally valid for all cultures, all nations, and all time. As we read the Bible from Genesis to Revelation, not as a series of isolated, disconnected stories and teachings but as a book with a single, comprehensive worldview, our minds are transformed. The Bible is no ordinary book. It holds divine power. "For the word of God is living and active. Sharper than any double-edged sword, it penetrates even to dividing soul and spirit, joints and marrow; it judges the thoughts and attitudes of the heart" (Heb. 4:12).

Third, God's Holy Spirit fills us and guides us to the truth. "But when he, the Spirit of truth, comes, he will guide you into all truth" (John 16:13). We have a live-in teacher with supernatural power who can reveal the truth to us.

Even with these benefits, we still have a responsibility. We cannot have a biblical worldview or a transformed mind if we spend most of our waking hours watching television, reading books, working, shopping, and in the process, ignoring Scripture. We must discipline ourselves to study and apply God's Word. As we do, our motivation is to bring glory and honor to God, and we honor him as we seek to love him with our entire mind.

Living It Out

Although God calls us to be holy and set apart, he also asks us to engage the world as his ambassadors (2 Cor. 5:20). Jesus says, "My prayer is not that you take them out of the world but that you protect them from the evil one. They are not of the world, even as I am not of it" (John 17:15–16). These words establish a tender balance. We are to be *in* the world, but not *of* the world. We are to be like a boat that is both in the water, yet sealed off from the water on the outside. It is our responsibility to disciple the nations (Matt. 28:18–20), and to do this, we engage with the nations. Yet at the same time, we are to be separate from the world by our determined allegiance to a biblical worldview.

To build the biblical worldview into your life, start where you are. Some may think this worldview requires that they quit their "secular" jobs and go into "full-time Christian service" meaning the pastorate or the mission field. "Full-time Christian service" however, is any service—any work—that is done to the glory of God and the good of others. Truth is needed everywhere, in every segment of society. When Jesus commands his followers to "make disciples of all nations" (Matt. 28:19), he also means we must take the biblical worldview to our own culture. Beginning with our current jobs and locations, we can take the truth into the marketplace and public arena. In the process, neighborhoods, communities, social institutions, and eventually laws and structures will change.

The biblical worldview has the power to transform lives and entire nations. Christ calls us to take this majestic worldview into our neighborhoods, communities, and nations.

DISCOVERY QUESTIONS
Sanctify Them by the Truth

The following verses and questions can help as you begin putting on the biblical worldview and living according to it.

1. Read 2 Corinthians 10:3–5. What imagery does the apostle Paul use in these verses, and why do you think this is important?

    _____

    _____

    _____

2. With these weapons, what are we seeking to demolish? What are we to take captive?

    _____

    _____

    _____

3. Read 1 Peter 1:13–16. What does the apostle Peter say we should prepare for action?

    _____

    _____

4. In verses 15–16 Peter challenges us to be holy. To be holy means to be set apart for God's purposes. How does holiness relate to what we've learned about "putting on" and "putting off" in this session?

    _____

    _____

    _____

5. Read John 17:13–19. How does Jesus describe God's Word?

    _____

    _____

6. Read the following passages. How are we to view the world and our relationship to it?

    John 15:18–19

    _____

    _____

Romans 12:2

_____

_____

Ephesians 2:1–2

_____

_____

Colossians 3:1–2

_____

_____

James 1:27; 4:4

_____

_____

1 John 2:15–17

_____

_____

7. Read the following passages. How else are we to view the world and our relationship to it?

    John 1:29; 3:16–17; 4:42; 8:12

    _____

    _____

    Acts 1:8

    _____

    _____

    2 Corinthians 5:18–20

    _____

    _____

John 17:15

_____

_____

Revelation 11:15

_____

_____

8. Read Acts 26:19–20. The words *repent* and *repentance* in this passage derive from the Greek word *metanoeo*, which is the root for the English word *metamorphosis*, or transformation. To repent literally means to have our thinking transformed. It means to "change your mind" or to be "re-minded." What are we to have our minds changed from? What are we to have them changed to?

_____

_____

9. Read Acts 17:10–12. Why were the Bereans of a "more noble character than the Thessalonians?" What were they seeking? How did they seek it?

_____

_____

10. How can you develop a Berean spirit?

_____

_____

KEY POINTS TO REMEMBER
A Final Review

1. "Putting off" false beliefs and "putting on" the truth contained in the biblical worldview does not happen automatically at conversion. It is a lifelong process that requires disciplined study of God's Word.

2. To love God "with all your mind" involves uncovering unconsciously held assumptions and exposing them to the light of Scripture. As we engage in this process, our minds are transformed, and transformed minds naturally lead to a transformation in our behavior and, ultimately, our entire lives.

3. God helps us in this process in three important ways: First, he works a remarkable transformation in our lives when we come to faith in Christ. Second, he provides us with his powerful, inspired Word in Scripture. Third, he sends his Holy Spirit to live within us to guide us in the truth.

4. We are to be "salt and light" by taking the biblical worldview out into our neighborhoods, communities, and nations. As we do, our cultures are transformed and our nations are discipled.

CLOSING THOUGHTS
Coram Deo

During the Reformation in Europe, many Christians used a motto to describe what we considered in this session. That motto was *coram Deo*, a Latin phrase meaning "before the face of God." For these Christians, all of life was lived "before the face of God." Life was not compartmentalized into spiritual, secular, or other categories. Even the most mundane tasks were charged with dynamism and meaning because believers understood and applied God's truth to every area of their lives.

Our challenge is to recapture this same spirit of *coram Deo* in our own generation. We need to view all of life through the lenses ground according to God's prescription. We need to regain a distinctly Christian mind. We need to begin acquiring and living with a biblical worldview, and this is a discipline.

Here are some ideas that can help you along in the process.

♦ Read the Bible from Genesis to Revelation to discover the major themes and basic presuppositions of Scripture.

♦ Observe how much time you spend reading and studying the Bible compared to watching television, reading magazines, or being involved in activities that feed you the assumptions of the dominant worldview in your culture.

◆ Develop a biblical perspective on your vocation. Read the Bible to see what it says about work.

◆ Read contemporary authors whose thinking is based in a biblical worldview.

◆ Read classic literature, written when Christians were intentionally writing from a biblical worldview perspective.

◆ Meet with like-minded Christians. Encourage one another to put on and live out the biblical worldview in all areas of your lives.

Let us commit ourselves to confidently taking the incomparable worldview of Scripture—the transforming story of the coming of God's kingdom—into our nations. And as the apostle Peter encourages us, may we "prepare our minds for action" (1 Pet. 1:13) as we confront and challenge false worldview assumptions in all aspects of society.

PERSONAL APPLICATION
You Can Put On a Biblical Worldview

Use the questions below to consider how to apply biblical truth in your life, family, vocation, and church.

1. One of the first areas to apply biblical truth is within our families. Consider or discuss the dominant view of family life in your society. How does it define the following?

The roles of husband and wife

_____

_____

The roles and value of children and teens

_____

_____

The roles and values of parents

_____

_____

Attitudes towards sexuality

_____

_____

2. Compare and contrast this dominant view with the biblical view in Scripture. If there are differences, what are they? Cite passages and verses that support the biblical perspective.

_____

_____

_____

_____

3. Consider your attitudes and beliefs about family life. Are there areas where you need to "repent" or change your thinking? If so, what are they? Be as specific as possible.

_____

_____

_____

4. Biblical truth can also be applied through your vocation and occupation. Which of the three quotations do you think best describes the view of "work" that the majority of people in your society hold?

> Wherever man may stand, whatever he may do, to whatever he may apply his hand, in agriculture, in commerce, and in industry, or his mind, in the world of art, and science he is, in whatsoever it may be, constantly standing before the face of God, he is employed in the

service of his God, he has strictly to obey his God, and above all, he has to aim at the glory of his God.

—*Abraham Kuyper*[8]

For me "work" is like an enemy.
All work, I'll leave it to the ox,
because God made work as a punishment.
...I like to dance merengue. Merengue's better than work
because having to work, it causes me great pain.

—*From a Latin American folk song*[9]

I work so I can consume—so I can have material things and live "the good life." I evaluate the success of my career in terms of upward mobility, increasing affluence, and increasing levels of consumption.

—*From* Lifework: Developing a Biblical Theology of Vocation[10]

5. What's your personal understanding of work? What do you need to do to bring your understanding of work more in line with the biblical worldview? Be specific.

6. Another area in which to apply the biblical worldview is through the ministry of your local church. What is your society's dominant view of the church?

7. What does the dominant view of your particular Christian tradition or denomination say about the role of the church?

    _____

    _____

    _____

8. In light of what you've learned about the biblical worldview in this study, has your understanding of the role of the church changed? If so, how? What do you think God may be calling you to do through your church?

    _____

    _____

    _____

    _____

    _____

    _____

A PRACTICAL RESPONSE

Making a New Beginning

Often a simple ceremony with symbolic meaning can carve a new spiritual pathway for us. So at the end of this session, consider joining together in a short ceremony that allows group members to commit to living out the implications of the biblical worldview in all areas of life. If you're studying alone, you can alter the activity accordingly.

Leaders, begin by asking individual members to draw or write on a piece of paper the components of their worldview in the past. Then, on a separate sheet of paper, have them indicate the components of a biblical worldview that they want to follow now.

Once all participants have finished the two papers, follow these steps.

1. Have them form a circle.
2. Ask them to first hold up their lists or drawings of their past worldviews. Either aloud or privately, they can confess to God the lies they've believed in the past about worldview.

3. Once they've confessed to God, ask group members to tear up their past worldviews and drop the pieces in a wastepaper can or bag.
4. Now ask them to hold up their sheets with a biblical worldview. Again, aloud or privately, they can commit this renewed outlook to God. Encourage them to keep this list as a reminder and for reference.
5. Close this session with a prayer of blessing from the leader or a selected group member. This person could also read Psalm 19:7–14 as a benediction.

Endnotes

Foreword

1. John R. W. Stott, *New Issues Facing Christians Today* (London: Marshall Pickering, 1999), p. 35.

Introduction

1. Thomas A. Bloomer, *A Biblical Worldview: The Wisdom and Foolishness of God and the Strength and Weakness of God*, Diss.: Trinity International University, 1997, p. 7.
2. Charles Colson and Nancy Pearcey, *How Now Shall We Live?* (Wheaton, Ill.: Tyndale House Publishers, Inc., 1999), pp. 14–15.
3. Ibid., p. 15.
4. Darrow L. Miller, *Discipling Nations: The Power of Truth to Transform Cultures* (Seattle: YWAM Publishing, 1998), p. 24.
5. Colson and Pearcey, *How Now Shall We Live?* p. 33.

Session 1

1. Josie Kornegay, staff person with YWAM Mercy Ships; interview by Darrow Miller, 1994.
2. This definition is similar to the one presented by James W. Sire in *The Universe Next Door* (Downers Grove, Ill.: InterVarsity Press, 1976), p. 17.
3. Samuel P. Huntington, *The Clash of Civilizations and the Remaking of World Order* (New York: Touchstone, 1996), p. 30.
4. Charles Colson and Nancy Pearcey, *How Now Shall We Live* (Wheaton, Ill.: Tyndale House Publishers, Inc., 1999), p. 13.
5. James W. Sire, *How to Read Slowly* (Wheaton, Ill.: Harold Shaw, 1978), pp. 14–15.
6. Colson and Pearcey, *How Now Shall We Live?* p. 34.

Session 2

1. Marvin Olasky, *The Tragedy of American Compassion* (Wheaton, Ill.: Crossway Books, 1992), p. 126.
2. *New York Courier and Enquirer*, April 16, 1847 (hereafter noted as *Courier*).
3. *Courier*, March 5, 1847.

4. *Courier*, April 16, 1847.
5. Olasky, *Tragedy of American Compassion*, pp. 170–71.
6. James T. Patterson, *America's Struggle Against Poverty, 1900–1985* (Cambridge, Mass.: Harvard University Press, 1986), p. 174.

Session 3

1. Carl Sagan, "Episode 1: The Shores of the Cosmic Ocean," *Cosmos*, VHS (Turner Home Entertainment, 1989).
2. This definition was informed by J. I. Packer in "Trinity: God Is One and Three" in his *Concise Theology: A Guide to Historic Christian Beliefs* (Wheaton Ill.: Tyndale House Publishers, Inc., 1993), accessed through Logos Library System.
3. Nancy R. Pearcey and Charles B. Thaxton, *The Soul of Science: Christian Faith and Natural Philosophy* (Wheaton, Ill,: Crossway Books, 1994) p. 25.
4. J. I. Packer, *Knowing God* (Downers Grove, Ill.: InterVarsity Press, 1973), p. 13.
5. Charles Colson and Nancy Pearcey, *How Now Shall We Live?* (Wheaton, Ill.: Tyndale House Publishers, Inc., 1999), p. 15.
6. Richard Lewontin as quoted by Phillip E. Johnson in "The Unraveling of Scientific Materialism," *First Things*, 77 (November, 1997), pp. 22–25.

Session 4

1. Malcolm Muggeridge, *Something Beautiful for God: Mother Teresa of Calcutta* (New York: Ballantine Books, 1971), p. 15.
2. Mother Teresa, *Words to Love By* (Notre Dame, Ind.: Ave Maria Press, 1983), p. 80.
3. Rodney Stark, *The Rise of Christianity: A Sociologist Reconsiders History* (Princeton, N.J.: Princeton University Press, 1996), pp. 214–15.
4. "The Image of God," *Tabletalk* from Ligonier Ministries and R. C. Sproul, Dec. 2001, p. 29.
5. Muggeridge, *Something Beautiful*, p. 16.
6. John R. W. Stott, *New Issues Facing Christians Today* (London: Marshall Pickering, 1999), p. 37.
7. Horace Greeley, *Hints Towards Reforms* (New York: Harper and Bros., 1850), p. 86.
8. William Provine, "Evolution: Free will and punishment and meaning in life" (lecture, University of Tennessee, Knoxville, February 12, 1998). Abstract of lecture accessed at http://eeb.bio.utk.edu/darwin/DarwinDayProvineAddress.htm.

9. Stott, *New Issues Facing Christians Today.*

10. Neale Donald Walsch, "Considering Religion," June 24, 2002 (an archived message on the website Conversations with God, http://www.cwg.org/en /10/10-10-20-10-archives/10-10-20-10-01.html).

Session 5

1. Much of the information on George Washington Carver was provided by Iowa State University's e-Library Special Collections Department. www.lib. iastate.edu/spcl/gwc.home.html

2. John S. Ferrell, *Fruits of Creation: A Look at Global Sustainability as Seen Through the Eyes of George Washington Carver* (Shakopee, Minn.: Macalester Park Publishing Company, 1995), p. 62.

3. Ibid.

4. Ibid., p. 50.

5. Michael Novak, *The Spirit of Democratic Capitalism* (New York: Simon & Schuster Publishers, 1982), p. 103.

6. J. I. Packer, "Creation: God Is the Creator," *Concise Theology: A Guide to Historic Christian Beliefs* (Wheaton, Ill.: Tyndale House Publishers, Inc., 1993), accessed through Logos Library System.

7. Osiyo Tsaligi Oginalii, "Healing Mother Earth," http://members.tripod.com /~Labyrinth_3/page15.html.

8. David M. Graber, "Mother Nature as a Hothouse Flower," (book review of *The End of Nature* by Bill McKibben) *Los Angeles Times,* Los Angeles, Calif.: Oct 22, 1989, pg. 1, ProQuest document ID: 66580324.

9. Carl Sagan, "Episode 1: The Shores of the Cosmic Ocean," *Cosmos,* VHS (Turner Home Entertainment, 1989).

Session 6

1. Thomas Cahill, *The Gift of the Jews* (New York: Nan A. Talese, 1998), p. 63.

2. Ibid., p. 64.

3. James W. Sire, *The Universe Next Door* (Downers Grove, Ill.: InterVarsity Press, 1976) p. 40.

4. Carl Sagan, "Episode 1: The Shores of the Cosmic Ocean," *Cosmos,* VHS (Turner Home Entertainment, 1989).

5. C. S. Lewis, *Christian Reflections* (Grand Rapids: W. B. Eerdmans Pub. Co., 1967), p. 105.

6. *The Columbia World of Quotations,* New York: Columbia University Press, 1996. www.bartleby.com/66/. [July 13, 2005].

7. Black Elk and John Gneisenau Neihardt, *Black Elk Speaks* (Lincoln: University of Nebraska Press, 1961), pp. 198–199.

Session 7

1. George Barna and Mark Hatch, *Boiling Point: Monitoring Cultural Shifts in the Twenty-First Century* (Ventura, Calif.: Regal Books, 2001) pp. 189, 192.
2. Based on numbers and estimates reported by the Alan Guttmacher Institute, www.agi-usa.org.
3. Barna Research Group Online, www.barna.org ©1995–2002 Barna Research Ltd.
4. Barna and Hatch, *Boiling Point*, p. 80.
5. E. Stanley Jones, *The Unshakable Kingdom and the Unchanging Person* (Nashville, Tenn.: Abingdon Press, 1972), p. 174.
6. Gailyn Van Rheenen, *Communicating Christ in Animistic Contexts* (Pasadena, Calif.: William Carey Library, 1991), p. 101.

Session 8

1. Os Guiness, *The Call: Finding and Fulfilling the Central Purpose of Your Life* (Nashville, Tenn.: Word Publishing, 1998), p. 28.
2. Ibid.
3. Ibid, p. 29
4. Ibid, p. 27
5. Ibid.
6. Spartacus Educational, http://www.spartacus.schoolnet.co.uk /REwilberforce.htm.
7. John R. W. Stott, *New Issues Facing Christians Today* (London: Marshall Pickering, 1999), p. 37.
8. Abraham Kuyper, *The Crown of Christian Heritage*, originally published as *Lectures on Calvinism* (Grand Rapids, Mich.: Wm. B. Eerdmans Publishing Company, 1931), p. 54.
9. Disciple Nations Alliance Online Course, http://www.disciple-nations.org /course/applife/course.php?a=3-2
10. Ibid.

~ Leader's Guide

We suggest the following guidelines for people leading study groups through this Bible study. Of course you will need to adapt the studies and our suggestions to your particular group and culture.

Preparing for and Facilitating a Group

◆ We suggest meeting for one hour per session. This will allow:
  ❖ 20 minutes to review the Key Verses and Biblical Insights sections.
  ❖ 20 minutes to discuss the Discovery Questions and Personal Application sections.
  ❖ 10 minutes to pray for one another.
  ❖ 10 minutes for general prayer and worship.
◆ To ensure that everyone contributes to the conversation, it's best to keep the group at six to eight participants (no more than twelve). If the membership increases, consider splitting into smaller groups during the discussion times and coming back together for concluding prayer.
◆ If group members have their own books, ask them to complete the session individually before they attend the meeting.
◆ To guide the group effectively, complete each session yourself before you meet together. Make sure you understand the main points of each session. Think about how they apply to your own life. Then, as you lead the group, you can better facilitate the discussion by clarifying the questions when needed and offering suggestions if the conversation lags.
◆ For each session, before you meet together, read through the Practical Response ideas at the end of the lesson. If you plan to complete one or more of the activities as a group, bring any necessary supplies to the meeting.
◆ For each meeting, arrive ahead of time to prepare the location (chairs, refreshments, teaching aids, etc.) and to greet group members as they arrive.

- For your first meeting, be sure to take time to introduce each group member. You may wish to do an activity that will help group members get to know each other. Introduce the study by presenting key ideas from the Introduction and reading the overall objectives for the sessions (listed in the Study Notes following this Leader's Guide).
- Be a *facilitator*, not a teacher. Here are some suggestions:
  - Encourage group participation. Sitting in a circle (rather than rows) can help.
  - Use group members' names.
  - Ask different people to pray and read.
  - Ask questions and wait for answers. Don't immediately give your own answer.
  - Thank group members for their ideas, and ask others what they think.
  - Draw out members who aren't contributing much.
  - Tactfully redirect the focus from participants who tend to dominate the discussion.
  - Ask participants for explanation when they give simple "yes" or "no" answers.
  - Pace your study at a rate that allows for group members' maximum understanding. Review as often as necessary.
  - Keep the session objective in mind as you work through the session. These objectives, as well as possible responses for questions, are listed in the Study Notes.

Suggestions for Leading Each Session

- Have a group member open and close each meeting time with prayer.
- Begin the meeting by reviewing the Key Points to Remember from the previous session. Take time to discuss how group members may have applied the teaching from the previous session since the last meeting.
- You may wish to assign the Key Verses to Read as a memorization exercise. If so, take time at the beginning of the session to allow group members to recite the verses corresponding to the session. This can easily be done in pairs to save time.

◆ Refer back to the Key Words to Know section as necessary during discussion.

◆ Read the Key Verses to Read and answer the questions provided as a group. (See possible responses to these questions in the Study Notes.)

◆ If each group member has a book, take turns reading the Biblical Insights section together. If you're the only one with a book, share the main points or read this section to the group. The Key Points to Remember section will help present the main ideas.

◆ Answer the Discovery Questions together as a group. (See possible responses to these questions in the Study Notes.)

◆ Answer the Personal Application questions together as a group. If group members have their own books, you may wish to break up into smaller groups (two to three people) and have each subgroup read and answer the Personal Application questions.

◆ Work on a Practical Response activity if you've chosen to do so. These optional ideas are provided to help group members apply the session's main points in their own lives.

◆ You will find the session Objectives, Possible Responses to Questions for Key Verses to Read, and Possible Responses to Discovery Questions for each session in the Study Notes that follow this Leader's Guide.

⤳ Study Notes

Whether you lead or participate in a small group or study alone, you may find it helpful to consult the session objectives and suggested responses for each session's Key Verses to Read and Discovery questions. Not all questions have a "right" or "wrong" answer, but these suggestions will help stimulate your thinking.

Session 1: What Is a Worldview?

Objective: To define *worldview* and examine its application to Christ's followers

Possible Responses to Questions for Key Verses to Read

1. Love the Lord your God with all your heart and with all your soul and with all your mind.
2. In the Bible the "heart" refers to our will, which is our innermost core—the center of our selves. To love God with all our hearts, therefore, is to submit our will completely to his will. It is to say with Jesus, "not my will, but yours be done" (Luke 22:42).
3. Our "mind" is the center of rationality and encompasses our thought life. To love God with all our mind requires us to "take captive every thought to make it obedient to Christ" (2 Cor. 10:5).
4. God has made us with both hearts and minds. Total devotion to God requires every part of us to be submitted to his lordship. If we fail to love God with all of our heart, our relationship with him may be little more than "head knowledge" with scant effect on our choices, emotions, and will. If we fail to love God with our entire mind, our relationship with him may be heartfelt and sincere but not based on the truth.

Possible Responses to Discovery Questions

1. Jesus and his disciples are on the winding mountain road that leads from Jericho to Jerusalem. It is Jesus' last trip to Jerusalem, and he is preparing the disciples for his imminent rejection and crucifixion.

2. James and John asked Jesus to do whatever they wanted, then asked him to give them places of honor, saying, "Let one of us sit at your right and the other at your left in your glory."

3. Jesus said that their request wasn't his to grant and that the places they sought "belong to those for whom they have been prepared."

4. They were filled with anger and jealousy. They "became indignant."

5. According to worldly standards, "great people" such as rulers and high officials "lord it over" their subordinates and "exercise authority over them."

6. According to Christ's standard of greatness, "Whoever wants to be first must be slave of all."

7. He did not come to be served.

8. He came "to serve, and to give his life as a ransom for many."

9. See the chart below.

	The Disciples' View	**Jesus' View (Reality)**
Who is Christ?	A political leader who will expel the Romans and re-establish Jewish sovereignty	The Son of God sent to the world to die on a cross to provide atonement for the sins of the world
What is the kingdom?	The kingdom is an earthly, political kingdom.	The kingdom is God's eternal reign over all creation.
What will the disciples' future lives be like?	They will rule with Jesus and hold positions of political power and authority.	They will suffer persecution and die for the sake of the gospel.
How should we live?	We should seek positions of power and authority and "lord it over" others.	We should seek to sacrificially serve others and give our lives for the sake of the gospel.

10. The disciples' false view was challenged (1) when Jesus was crucified and (2) when he rose from the grave, appeared to them, and gave them the Great Commission (Matt. 28:18–20).

Session 2: Worldviews at Work in the World

Objective: To review the dominant worldviews in the world and how they function in shaping culture

Possible Responses to Questions for Key Verses to Read

1. Proverbs 2:6 says, "the Lord gives wisdom...knowledge and understanding." Proverbs 3:13 says, "blessed is the man who finds wisdom."
2. We ought to love wisdom and seek it.
3. "Hollow and deceptive"
4. "Human tradition and the basic principles of this world"
5. The elementary building blocks of any culture that are based on satanic deceptions rather than on the truth

Possible Responses to Discovery Questions

1. God's "word is truth." God "speak[s] the truth" and "declare[s] what is right." All truth originates with him.
2. By holding to Jesus' teaching and learning from him
3. From "the basic principles of the world"
4. "Truth came through Jesus Christ." Jesus said, "I am the...truth." He said, "For this reason I was born, and for this I came into the world, to testify to the truth. Everyone on the side of truth listens to me." We can know the truth by listening to Jesus and the testimony of his life, death, and resurrection.
5. The Holy Spirit is the "Spirit of truth" who "guide[s] you into all truth."
6. Scripture reveals truth as something that is objectively real. It is revealed by God through his Word, through Christ, and through the Holy Spirit. It can be sought, discovered, and understood.
7. People can know the truth through observing creation (Rom. 1:18–20), through their consciences (Rom. 2:15), through the life and teachings of Jesus (John 1:1–3; 14), and through the Bible (2 Tim. 3:16).
8. The Bible instructs us to choose truth, set our hearts on it, buy it and not sell it, seek it, and love it.

9. By searching the Scriptures
10. Please write this in your own words.

Session 3: The Truth about Ultimate Reality

Objective: To understand some critical foundational beliefs of the Christian worldview (the worldview of the kingdom of God) and the impact these beliefs can have on our everyday lives

Possible Responses to Questions for Key Verses to Read

1. God
2. He created the heavens and the earth, revealing that he is a creative being.
3. The universe originated with God. He is "before all things, and in him all things hold together" (Col. 1:17). Everything that exists owes its existence to God and is contingent on him.

Possible Responses to Discovery Questions

1. God the Father and God the Son both existed before the creation of the world, as did the Spirit (Gen. 1:2). In John 17:24, we also see that personality, relationship, and love all existed before the creation of the universe.
2. God is full of love. He desires to love us and make himself known to us.
3. His love toward us is great. It is a sacrificial, giving, other-oriented love.
4. "God demonstrates his own love for us in this: While we were still sinners, Christ died for us" (Rom. 5:8).
5. "Jesus Christ laid down his life for us. And we ought to lay down our lives for our brothers. If anyone has material possessions and sees his brother in need but has no pity on him, how can the love of God be in him? Dear children, let us not love with words or tongue but with actions and in truth" (1 John 3:16–18).
6. If God were merciful but not just, there would be no foundation for justice and the punishment of evil. If God were just but not merciful,

there would be no foundation for mercy and forgiveness. Because God is both just and merciful, there exists a tender balance between mercy and forgiveness on one hand, and justice and the punishment of evil on the other. We need both in a fallen world.

7. God is perfect, faithful, just, upright, righteous, and holy. He stands against all unrighteousness and wickedness.

8. Wickedness, godlessness, and the suppression of truth

9. God created the heavens and earth "in wisdom" and "by his understanding." He created them according to his purpose and design. The universe is not random or chaotic but displays evidence of design. This design reveals God's existence, power, and divinity.

10. Diversity is affirmed because God created both male and female, each with diverse gifts and abilities. Unity is affirmed because through marriage, the two are united and become "one flesh."

11. Diversity is affirmed because there are different kinds of "gifts," "service," and "working." Unity is affirmed because there is one Spirit and one God who supplies them all.

12. Unity and diversity can be affirmed in the relationship that exists between nations and cultures. Each culture has unique features that include language, customs, and values. Yet all share a core of unity because God creates men and women from all nations in his image (Gen. 1:27).

Session 4: A Biblical Look at Humanity

Objective: To understand some critical foundational beliefs of the Christian view of humanity and the impact these beliefs can have on our everyday lives

Possible Responses to Questions for Key Verses to Read

1. Humanity is different from the rest of creation because it is created in God's image. Humanity is similar to the rest of creation because it is also created by God.

2. God is spirit (John 4:24) and does not dwell in a body, so bearing his image does not refer to physical resemblances. Rather, we resemble

God's nonphysical qualities and abilities, for example, the fact that he is a moral being, is relational, and can love, think, reflect, create, and choose. Because God created us in his image, all human life is endowed with inherent worth and dignity. In other words, human life is sacred.

3. According to this passage, one of God's purposes in creating humanity was for them to "rule...over all the earth" under his supreme authority.

4. Both male and female are of equal value and worth in God's sight.

Possible Responses to Discovery Questions

1. "You made [man] a little lower than the heavenly beings and crowned him with glory and honor. You made him ruler over the works of your hands; you put everything under his feet" (Ps. 8). According to Psalm 139, mankind is "fearfully and wonderfully made" by God who "knit me together in my mother's womb." Likewise, "all the days ordained for me were written in your book before one of them came to be."

2. God values human life so much that "he gave his one and only Son" (John 3:16) to die for us, so that we may enjoy eternal life with him. He values each person and wants "everyone to come to repentance" (2 Pet. 3:9).

3. Mankind was "created in the likeness of God...male and female." This is the core unity among all people, that we share in "the likeness of God."

4. People from all nations descend from the same ancestors, Adam and Eve. We have the same blood in our veins. This establishes equality among people and nations. God desires for people from all nations to "seek him...and reach out for him and find him."

5. God put Adam and Eve in the Garden of Eden "to work it and take care of it." Work is a blessing from God. He made us creative, working beings. However, the Fall affected our work, making it "painful toil" (Gen. 3:17). Still, work is not a curse. It is a blessing from God. We discover purpose and meaning in life, in part, through our work.

6. Ants are diligent, hardworking creatures. We ought to apply these same virtues to our work. Like ants, we can save for the future. If we

do, we'll be less likely to fall into poverty. "All hard work brings profit, but mere talk [laziness] leads to poverty."

7. Please answer this question from your own experience.
8. The wickedness of humanity is "great" (Gen. 6:5). Rom. 1:28–32 informs us that fallen man has "a depraved mind, [and does] what ought not to be done." They have "become filled with every kind of wickedness, evil, greed and depravity. They are full of envy, murder, strife, deceit and malice. They are gossips, slanderers, God-haters, insolent, arrogant and boastful; they invent ways of doing evil; they disobey their parents; they are senseless, faithless, heartless, ruthless."
9. It stirs up his wrath (Rom. 1:18).
10. No one is righteous. "All have sinned and fall short of the glory of God" (Rom. 3:23). Human righteousness is "like filthy rags" in God's sight (Isa. 64:6).
11. There is hope for redemption through faith in Christ Jesus. "God presented him as a sacrifice of atonement" and our sins are forgiven "through faith in his blood" (Rom. 3:25).

Session 5: The Glory of Creation

Objective: To understand some critical foundational beliefs of the Christian view of creation and the impact these beliefs can have on our everyday lives

Possible Responses to Questions for Key Verses to Read

1. God blessed Adam and Eve through relationships with himself, each other, and creation. He placed them in a beautiful garden. They could enjoy both its beauty and bounty. He blessed them by granting them dominion over creation. They could enjoy meaningful work by discovering creation's hidden secrets, caring for creation, and participating in the expansion of God's creation as it filled the earth.
2. He commanded them to (1) "be fruitful and increase in number," (2) "fill the earth and subdue it," and (3) "rule over...every living creature."
3. He gave them "every seed-bearing plant...and every tree that has fruit." God gave them these for their food.

4. God described all he had made as "very good." This is not a relative value but an eternal value assigned by the Creator. Creation reflects God's wisdom and goodness. There is nothing in creation that is not good. God created everything and desires everything to be redeemed from the effects of the Fall (Col. 1:16, 19–20).

Possible Responses to Discovery Questions

1. Through his spoken Word
2. For both God and humans, the act of creating begins in the mind/spirit. Like God, we imagine things before they exist tangibly. Unlike God, we are not able to create by our spoken word. We cannot create *ex nihilo* (out of nothing) as God can. Rather, we take the materials of creation and develop new innovations.
3. The visible or the tangible comes from the invisible. This is true with God and with people. The act of creating begins with the invisible, that is, with the mind/spirit.
4. The natural laws that govern the physical universe, electricity, the periodic table of elements, the uniformity and regularity of motion of the planets and stars, etc.
5. Please answer this in your own words.
6. Genesis 1:28 indicates that God intended for Eden to be a starting point, not an ending point. God created Adam and Eve with the ability to reproduce and commanded them to do so, saying, "Be fruitful and increase in number; fill the earth" (Gen. 1:28). God also created the natural world with the same ability to reproduce. With regard to plants, he said, "Let the land produce vegetation: seed-bearing plants and trees on the land that bear fruit with seed in it, according to their various kinds" (Gen. 1:11). Likewise, after creating the sea creatures and birds, God said, "Be fruitful and increase in number and fill the water in the seas, and let the birds increase on the earth" (Gen. 1:22). These same commands to reproduce and fill the earth are restated after the Flood (Gen. 9:1).
7. He desires for the world to be filled with living creatures and people.
8. God desires that the whole earth be "filled with the knowledge of the glory of the LORD" (Hab. 2:14), which is revealed, in part, through his

creation. Creation reveals the glory, wisdom, power, and majesty of the Creator, showing us God's invisible, eternal qualities.

9. Psalm 8 declares, "You made [humanity] ruler over the works of your hands; you put everything under his feet." Man exercises dominion over God's creation under God's supreme authority. Creation belongs to God, not people. It is "the work of God's hands." Man has a delegated authority over creation and is accountable to God for how he exercises this authority.

10. On the part of God, it reveals the heart of a servant. God could have named the animals and declared to Adam, "You call them what I tell you to call them." Instead, he gave Adam the privilege of naming the animals. On the part of Adam, it reveals that he bears the image of God. Because God is creative, Adam is also creative. Adam stands apart from the rest of the created order as one who is able to use language and create names. God gave Adam the privilege of joining with him in the work of creation.

11. God put Adam and Eve in the Garden "to work it and take care of it" (Gen. 2:15).

12. Our dominion or authority over nature is to be marked by biblical stewardship. We are to tenderly care for creation.

13. God commanded that every seventh year they "let the land lie unplowed and unused." This cares for the land by allowing it to rest. It cares for the poor and the wild animals. It allows "the poor among [you to] get food from it (by gleaning), and the wild animals [to] eat what they leave" (Exod. 23:11).

Session 6: The Meaning of History

Objective: To understand some critical foundational beliefs of the Christian view of history and the impact these beliefs can have on our everyday lives

Possible Responses to Questions for Key Verses to Read

1. The "bride" is the church and the "husband" is Christ.

2. Unlike in the present-day Jerusalem, in the new Jerusalem God will "dwell" or "live with" his people. The church will experience an

intimacy with God that is impossible in the "old order" where sin and death exist. The new order will be without sorrow. God will wipe every tear from their eyes, and death with its mourning, pain, and crying will vanish.

3. God is Lord over the beginning and the end of history. He directs human history according to his purposes.

Possible Responses to Discovery Questions

1. God promised Abraham that he would make him a great nation, bless him, and make his name great. God promised to bless "all peoples on earth" through Abraham's descendants.

2. In this passage, people from "every nation, tribe, people, and language" praise Christ before his throne. They have been blessed because their sins were washed away by "the blood of the lamb." They will no longer hunger or thirst, and "God will wipe away every tear from their eyes."

3. They reveal that God has a plan he is unfolding for the redemption and restoration of creation—a plan with a definite beginning and end and which will surely be completed.

4. No. Like Abraham, God may give us a vision for the part that we are to play in his great plan. We are to faithfully do our part, without expecting that we will see the results or fruit of our labors in our lifetime.

5. The reward is God's esteem. He is "not ashamed to be called their God." Furthermore, God is preparing a heavenly home for them, a place of unimaginable rest, peace, and fulfillment.

6. As Christians we should have a linear perspective of time—a perspective of a real past, present, and future. We should understand time as the place where God is actively unfolding the events of our lives and of history to fulfill his perfect plans. This means that everything is significant and purposeful. It also means that there is real hope for a better future, so we need not get discouraged or lose heart. Paul and the writer of Hebrews were driven by the vision of a future prize or a goal. This prize is the believer's perfection and glorification—God's perfect intentions for our lives being fully realized and rewarded. The

imagery in these verses is of an athletic event in which racers are straining with all their might for victory. The racers are surrounded by a huge crowd of spectators (a "great cloud of witnesses") who have already completed the race and are cheering them onward. The racers are spurred by the memory of a great champion—Jesus Christ— who has gone before them and made it possible for them to compete because of his sacrifice.

7. The certainty of Christ's return should fill us with a reverent awe— that we ourselves will one day see our Redeemer. It should also fill us with a holy fear, because we know that when Christ returns, he will judge all people according to their deeds. Christ's certain return should make us people of hope, confident that God will fulfill his promises. And because we do not know exactly when Christ will return, we should live holy, godly lives in the present. Our actions should be pure and blameless. We should strive to be at peace with God.

8. The master is Jesus. The servants are his disciples.

9. The minas or talents represent the skills and spiritual gifts that Jesus has given his disciples. He wants them to "put [them] to work until I come back." When Jesus returns, he is going to ask his disciples "what they [have] gained" through using their talents, skills, and gifts.

10. He wants us to recognize our skills and talents as gifts from him and use them in service of his kingdom until he returns. He wants us to be active, creative, and diligent in using the gifts he has given us.

11. "Seven years of great abundance are coming throughout the land of Egypt, but seven years of famine will follow them. Then all the abundance in Egypt will be forgotten, and the famine will ravage the land" (Gen. 41:29–30). God had "firmly decided" to bring these events to pass.

12. He encouraged Pharaoh to take a fifth of the harvest of Egypt during the seven years of abundance and store it to be used during the seven years of famine.

13. God used Joseph to save people from many nations from starvation "because the famine was severe in all the world" (Gen. 41:37). God promised to bless the nations of the world through Abraham's descendants, and we see this occurring through this story. Even though God

is sovereign over the events of history, we should not be passive or fatalistic in how we live. We should prayerfully seek to understand God's plans to bless the nations and participate in them as Joseph did.

14. One person. God's kingdom advances through the faithful efforts of individuals. Individual lives count in God's plan for history.

Session 7: The ABCs of Culture

Objective: To understand that Satan is the father of lies and that his lies impact not only individuals but also entire communities and cultures; to identify and begin breaking free from Satan's cultural lies

Possible Responses to Questions on Key Verses to Read

1. Jesus describes Satan as "a murderer from the beginning, not holding to the truth, for there is no truth in him. When he lies, he speaks his native language, for he is a liar and the father of lies."
2. Deception
3. Lies
4. They become "enslaved."
5. Jesus describes himself as "the truth."

Possible Responses to Discovery Questions

1. Because they "suppress the truth by their wickedness."
2. The word *suppress* means to forcefully hold something back. It implies that the truth is not hidden or secret. People can readily know the truth. Instead of acknowledging the truth, however, fallen humanity suppresses it.
3. "God's invisible qualities—his eternal power and divine nature—have been clearly seen, being understood from what has been made" (Rom. 1:20).
4. "They neither glorified him as God nor gave thanks to him" (Rom. 1:21). As a result, "their thinking became futile and their...hearts were darkened.... They became fools" (Rom. 1:21–22).
5. "They did not think it worthwhile to retain the knowledge of God" (Rom. 1:28). As a result, "they have become filled with every kind of wickedness, evil, greed and depravity. They are full of envy, murder,

strife, deceit and malice. They are gossips, slanderers, God-haters, insolent, arrogant and boastful; they invent ways of doing evil; they disobey their parents; they are senseless, faithless, heartless, ruthless" (Rom. 1:29–30).

6. Please give your own opinion.

7. Our struggle is not against "flesh and blood." It's against "the rulers …the authorities [and] the powers of this dark world and against the spiritual forces of evil in the heavenly realms" (Eph. 6:12).

8. Please answer in your own words.

9. In these passages, Satan is described as "the devil," "the dragon," "that ancient serpent," and "the god of this age." He lies, leads the whole world astray, and deceives the nations.

10. Satan has blinded unbelievers to the truth of the gospel.

11. As one of slavery and bondage

12. He sent his Son to redeem us.

13. We are no longer slaves but are now adopted children and co-heirs with Christ.

14. The future choice for believers is to remain in our present freedom or to return once again to slavery.

15. We were enslaved "under the basic principles of the world" (Gal. 4:3).

16. We are set free if we "hold to" the teachings of Jesus.

17. We can stand against Satan's schemes by holding to the truth—the Word of God. The first item of armor is "the belt of truth."

Session 8: Putting on the Biblical Worldview

Objective: To commit to the discipline of living a life firmly rooted in biblical truth in all areas

Possible Responses to Questions for Key Verses to Read

1. We are to no longer conform "to the pattern of this world."

2. We are to be transformed "by the renewing of [our] mind."

3. As a result, we will "be able to test and approve what God's will is."

Possible Responses to Discovery Questions

1. He uses the imagery of war and battle. It's important because we are, quite literally, in a war against Satan.

2. "We demolish arguments and every pretension that sets itself up against the knowledge of God, and we take captive every thought to make it obedient to Christ" (2 Cor. 10:5).

3. Our minds

4. To be holy, or set apart for God's purposes, we put off the worldly mind-set of our culture and put on the biblical worldview. Holiness requires not only moral piety; it also requires that we "take captive every thought to make it obedient to Christ."

5. Jesus describes God's Word as truth.

6. We are to keep ourselves "from being polluted by the world." Friendship with the world makes us an enemy of God (James 1:27; 4:4). We are not to "love the world or anything in the world," for "the world and its desires pass away" (1 John 2:15–17).

7. God loves the world and sent his Son Jesus to "save the world." God is at work "reconciling the world to himself in Christ." He has given us a task in this work. He has given us the message of reconciliation, and we are to serve as ambassadors to the world with this message (2 Cor. 5:18–20). Jesus prays for us, not that we be taken out of the world, but that we be left in the world to serve as his witnesses to the world. He prays that we'll be protected from Satan (John 17:15).

8. We are to have our minds changed from ones that are based on the patterns of the world to ones that are thoroughly informed by biblical truth.

9. The Bereans were of a more noble character because they sought the truth by searching the Scriptures.

10. We need to develop the discipline of thinking critically so we can reject worldly ideas that come to us through our culture and replace them with the truth as revealed through our study of Scripture.

About the Authors

Darrow L. Miller is a vice president with Food for the Hungry International and cofounder of the Disciple Nations Alliance. He has served with FHI since 1981. His passion is helping people understand and apply the biblical worldview so that nations can be released from hunger and poverty. His book *Discipling Nations* (1998, YWAM Publishing) reveals his heart to renew the church's vision for discipling nations. Darrow has an M.A. in adult education. He has four grown children and lives with his wife, Marilyn, in Cave Creek, Arizona.

Bob Moffitt is president of the Harvest Foundation and co-founder of the Disciple Nations Alliance. For over thirty years he has developed and directed Christian organizations designed to encourage and enable Christians to demonstrate God's love, especially to broken people and their communities. He writes and teaches curricula designed to enable lay Christians to live out their faith in practical terms, particularly in the context of their local churches. He and his wife, Judy, live in Phoenix, Arizona.

Scott D. Allen is the worldwide coordinator of the Disciple Nations Alliance. He has served with Food for the Hungry International (FHI) since 1989, serving as Director of Human Resource Development. He has also served as a missionary in Japan, teaching English through local churches in the Osaka area. Scott has a bachelor's degree in history and education from Willamette University in Salem, Oregon. Scott lives with his wife, Kim, and their four children in Phoenix, Arizona.

Other KINGDOM LIFESTYLE Bible Studies

Revolutionizing Lives and Renewing Minds!

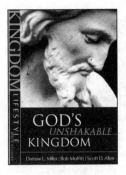

God's Unshakable Kingdom

by Scott D. Allen, Darrow L. Miller, and Bob Moffitt

The concept of the kingdom of God is one of the most confusing and misunderstood ideas in the Bible. Yet it's indisputable that the kingdom of God was central to Jesus' teachings. As he ministered, Jesus talked passionately about the kingdom. The phrase "kingdom of God" or "kingdom of heaven" appears ninety-eight times in the New Testament, more than sixty times on the lips of Jesus. This profound study explores the kingdom of God, helping believers build a biblical understanding of the vision for which Jesus lived and died—a vision that transforms individuals, families, churches, and whole nations.

ISBN 1-57658-346-5

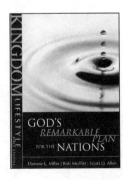

God's Remarkable Plan for the Nations

by Scott D. Allen, Darrow L. Miller, and Bob Moffitt

God's redemptive plan is the central theme of the entire Bible, from Genesis to Revelation. While this plan begins with individuals, it's more comprehensive—more wonderful—than this. God's redemptive interest extends to the healing and transformation of entire nations and cultures, undercutting injustice, poverty, and corruption and encompassing every sphere of society, from commerce to the arts to government. Will the church in our generation be faithful to Jesus' command to make disciples of all nations according to the fullness of what he intended? For this to occur, we must regain a comprehensive understanding of God's remarkable plan for the nations—a plan that touches your life profoundly.

ISBN 1-57658-352-X

Available at your local Christian bookstore or through YWAM Publishing
www.ywampublishing.com
1-800-922-2143

Disciple
Nations
Alliance

Founded by:
Harvest and Food for
the Hungry International

The Disciple Nations Alliance (DNA) is a global movement of individuals, churches, and organizations with a common vision: to see engaged, credible, high-impact local churches effecting real transformation in their communities and in sufficient mass to disciple their nations.

DNA was founded in 1997 through a partnership between Food for the Hungry and Harvest. Our mission is to envision churches with a biblical worldview and equip them to practice a wholistic, incarnational ministry affecting all spheres of society. We provide simple tools that enable churches to begin the transformation process immediately with existing resources—no matter how materially poor they may be.

If you would like more information about the Disciple Nations Alliance or our teaching and training resources, please visit our website: www.disciplenations.org.

Disciple Nations Alliance

1220 E. Washington Street
Phoenix, Arizona 85034
www.disciplenations.org

Founding Partners

Food for the Hungry International
www.fhi.net

Harvest Foundation
www.harvestfoundation.org

Samaritan Strategy Africa

The messages and teaching contained in the Kingdom Lifestyle Bible Studies are being championed throughout the continent of Africa through the efforts of Samaritan Strategy Africa, a collaborative network of African churches and Christian organizations that have banded together to accomplish the urgent goal of awakening, equipping, and mobilizing the African church to rise up and transform society. Through training, mentoring, conferences, and publications, Samaritan Strategy Africa aims to help churches

♦ discover God's vision of comprehensive healing and transformation of the nations;
♦ adopt a biblical worldview and then live it out by taking truth, goodness, and beauty into every sphere of society;
♦ practice a ministry of outreach within the community, demonstrating Christ's love to needy and broken people through works of service.

If you would like more information about Samaritan Strategy Africa or you would like to find out about upcoming training events or how you, your church, or your organization can be involved, we invite you to visit our website or contact us.

Samaritan Strategy Africa

Dennis Tongoi, Team Leader
PO Box 40360, 00100
Nairobi, Kenya
Phone: (254) 20-2720037/56
Email: afg@cms-africa.org
Website: www.samaritan-strategy-africa.org

Samaritan Strategy Africa is affiliated with the Disciple Nations Alliance (DNA), a global movement founded in 1997 through a partnership between Food for the Hungry and Harvest. DNA exists to see engaged, credible, high-impact local churches effecting real transformation in their communities and in sufficient mass to disciple their nations. For more information, visit www.disciplenations.org.